In Her Shoes

A Compilation of Inspiring Stories from the
First Decade of the
Worcester Women's Oral History
Project

Maureen Ryan Doyle
and
Charlene L. Martin

ISBN-13: 978-1517250980
ISBN-10: 1517250986

Cover Design by Breanna Goodrow

Photographs Provided by Interviewees

Konstantina Lukes Photo Credit: Michael D. Kane

Printed in the United States of America

Dedication

In memory of my father and mother, Joe and Mary Longhi, who taught me not to judge others because I don't know their stories.

Charlene L. Martin

To my mother, Mary Sweeney Ryan, for showing me that every woman is of value. And to my aunt, Edna Mae Sweeney, for teaching me that nothing is more fascinating than history.

Maureen Ryan Doyle

CONTENTS

ACKNOWLEDGMENTS

Our sincere and enduring gratitude is extended to Linda Rosenlund whose vision and hard work brought the Worcester Women's Oral History Project (WWOHP) to life; to Melanie Demarais for our nominations to the Steering Committee of the Worcester Women's History Project (WWHP) which started this journey for us; to the Schlesinger Library on the History of Women in America at the Radcliffe Institute of Harvard University, the official repository of the 300 WWOHP transcripts and recordings; to Kathryn Allamong Jacob, curator of manuscripts at the Schlesinger Library, for her ongoing encouragement; to Dr. Lisa Krissoff Boehm, oral historian and dean of the School of Arts and Sciences at Manhattanville College for her expertise and support of WWOHP; to William Wallace, executive director of the Worcester Historical Museum for providing a home for WWHP; to the members of the WWOHP subcommittee for their hard work and diligence; and to the members of WWHP and WWOHP whose mission it is to raise awareness of Worcester's unique role in the establishment of the Women's Rights Movement.

We thank the college professors who have incorporated oral history into their curricula. It is through their efforts and those of their students, that WWOHP has acquired most of its 300 archived oral histories of Worcester women. We are especially proud of the unique features of the collection including oral histories from Deaf women conducted in American Sign Language and Latina women in Spanish with English translation. A special thank you is given to Professor Judy Freedman Fask, former director of the Deaf Studies Program at College of the Holy Cross, for oversight of the interviews with Deaf women and assisting in the editing of those transcripts. We extend our gratitude also to Dr. Maryanne Leone and Dr. Esteban Loustaunau whose honors Spanish classes at Assumption College provided us with the interviews conducted in Spanish. Full transcripts in both English and Spanish are available on the WWHP website, www.wwhp.org along with many other full transcripts from the collection.

We thank all the women who agreed to have their life stories collected, preserved, and shared by WWOHP. The definition of history is changed forever by their courage and honesty.

Charlene would like to thank her husband, Jim, for *still* listening to her stories and her brother, John, who remembers all her stories from the "olden" days.

Maureen would like to thank her husband, Frank, who remains her greatest source of encouragement; and Colin and Dani Doyle who continue to surprise and inspire her on a daily basis.

FOREWORD

We cannot possibly predict all the things in life that will be presented to us. What we can do is to take every opportunity in stride, considering each fork in the road, and giving it our best.

It's common to hear the question, "What defines success in a woman's life?" There are many answers to this question, which create the illusion that it is a modern conundrum, but it is not. No matter what we have each experienced, one thing resonating with us as women is how content we are with the experiences, opportunities, challenges, and growth encountered in our respective lives when we reflect on our personal stories.

I am often asked to share my story and how I came to be where I am today. I am asked what advice I took, which quote inspired me, why I chose to run for office, or how I managed to attain a PhD and MBA with three children. Women who were products of the mid-twentieth century like myself were expected to be highly functioning wives, mothers, and if we had jobs, workers. We had no role models. Success was getting married and raising a family to the best of our abilities, and everything else that happened was serendipitous. We were pioneers and I did not map out my life; I just did my best to take advantage of every opportunity. I had motivation, persistence, and was willing to take risks. I was passionate about learning, teaching, and giving back to my community. When I look back on my journey, I see a road of cobblestones—different stones of various sizes fitted one after another.

I graduated from Wellesley College in an era where it was uncommon for women to pursue jobs apart from teaching, secretarial administration, or nursing. At that time, the Worcester Public School system had just begun hiring married women, so I landed a job as a teacher at North High School. Naturally, I was curious about the next step, which was to further my career in teaching. I enrolled at Clark University and the school allowed me the flexibility I needed to continue as a part-time doctoral student after I began having children. I was fortunate to receive support from the Radcliffe Institute that was willing to help women juggling family, education, and work. After receiving my PhD, I went on to pursue my MBA at Simmons School of Management. My MBA ultimately aided my transition into politics.

Since then, I have served as Massachusetts State Representative of the 13th Worcester District, and first woman from Worcester to hold the Massachusetts State Senate seat of the 1st Worcester District. I am currently the second woman in Massachusetts history to hold the State Senate Majority Leader seat. In each instance, I had to seize the opportunity when it appeared before me, move beyond my comfort zone, and recognize that much support was to be had, if I sought it.

It takes strength, openness, toughness, and risk to reach out for the opportunities in front of you. The women profiled in this book have undoubtedly sacrificed to get to where they are today, and I hope that as you continue reading, you are able to reflect on your own story and the journey that got you to where you are today. I hope that when you think of success and what defines it, that you do not dwell on the numerous thoughts of "if only" or anything that could, should, or would have been. As women, we are smart, resilient, compassionate, and conditioned to be multi-taskers. All things happen for reasons that we might not be able to understand at the moment. Later on, what remains will be what we truly believed in, how we stood for the things that mattered to us, and how we accomplished them. To me, that is a worthy definition of success.

Harriette L. Chandler
Massachusetts Senate
Majority Leader
September 1, 2015

INTRODUCTION

Don't judge a [wo]man until you have walked a mile in [her] shoes.

Native American proverb

The Worcester Women's History Project (WWHP) was established in 1994 to increase awareness of the prominent role Worcester, Massachusetts, played in the abolition and suffrage movements in the 19th century, and in particular to highlight the importance of the First National Woman's Rights Convention that was held in Worcester in 1850. Most historians point to the 1848 regional meeting at Seneca Falls, New York, as the origin of the Women's Rights Movement. Yet, it is the Worcester 1850 Convention that was the first organized and nationwide call to action.

The Worcester Women's Oral History Project (WWOHP) was launched in 2005 as a major initiative of WWHP. It records, collects, and shares the personal and historical memories of women from Central Massachusetts. In this way, it supports the mission of WWHP to not only celebrate the past achievements of Worcester women, but also to preserve the accomplishments of the current generation. WWOHP seeks to build community by sharing experiences through the collection of women's stories. Oral history is an excellent method to capture women's experiences. By sharing these stories of women from different generations, ethnicities, religions, and socio-economic backgrounds, we come to understand, that despite our differences, there are often common threads which unite all women.

At the time of publication, nearly 300 oral histories have been collected and transcribed. Many full-text transcripts are available to the public on the Project's website. The Project is honored to have the Schlesinger Library as the permanent repository for its oral histories. The Schlesinger Library on the History of Women in America is on the campus of Radcliffe Institute at Harvard University, and maintains collections relating to a wide range of American women's activities. It provides rich material for researchers and historians around the world.

The purpose of this book is not to replicate complete and unedited transcripts of oral histories, but rather to provide a window into the life and times of some of the women chronicled by WWOHP. Our aim is to condense stories without altering the facts, tone, or meaning of the original transcripts. Therefore, there may be slight variations between the recorded interviews and the stories that are printed here.

Selections for this book were not based on any presuppositions. We, the editors and co-chairpersons of WWOHP, found them interesting and relevant to women's varied experiences. In our first book, *Voices of Worcester Women: 160 Years after the First Woman's Rights Convention*, we focused on the issues pertinent to the 1850 Convention: education, health, work, and politics/community involvement. As we researched and reviewed the full transcripts for this book, certain common themes emerged. These are the topics of work/life balance, commitment, and the search to find one's own path in life. We grouped the excerpts accordingly.

Almost every woman who was interviewed discussed the high wire act of finding time for the competing responsibilities of spouses, children, parents, extended family, careers, housework, and volunteering.

The excerpts reflect the daily struggles of women from different backgrounds: professional and blue collar, those with children and those childfree, women who work at home and those who labor outside the home, those who have hired help and those without. The attempt to find a balance that suits each woman's priorities is both encouraging and awe-inspiring. If you have ever wondered, "How does she do it?" just take a peek into the chapter entitled Balancing Act.

Another universal theme which emerged is the passion the women displayed when talking about what is near and dear to them. Worcester women make many sacrifices, devoting time and energy to causes in which they believe. Often, they work or volunteer many hours to make their community and their world better places. In this chapter you will read about women working in politics, medicine, education, as well as social services to help the poor, immigrants, children, the environment, and other women.

The final chapter includes excerpts from women's stories of how they created their path in life. Some overcame the adversity of illness, poverty, teen pregnancy, loss of parents, sexual assault, or moving to a new country. Others tell of a non-traditional experience whether it is working in a male-dominated field, returning to college as an older adult, or choosing not to marry or not to have children. All describe a journey of self-discovery.

The lives of women are rich and complex, and so are their stories. We view the tapestry of 20th and 21st century America here—war; immigration; the Civil Rights Movement; the Women's Rights Movement; commitment to family, faith, and friends; the struggle to be independent and to be interdependent; and much more. We are invited into personal struggles and private triumphs. We engage these women, not through the prism of another's thoughts or words, but through their own words. For there is power in the word, and ultimate power in the word of the woman recounting the moments of her own life, the path that is hers and hers alone.

The organizers of the first Woman's Rights Convention held in Worcester all those years ago might be amazed to see the choices available to women today. Yet, women still face judgment and criticism over the choices they make. We applaud the women who shared their life stories with us. They are courageous, forthright, and honest. Perhaps there will be less judgment and more understanding in the world if more women told their stories. We hope this book reflects at least a slight movement in that direction.

In a culture that is driven daily by the power of celebrity, the day-to-day struggles, challenges, and victories of ordinary women in Central Massachusetts could be easily lost. However, these oral histories provide us, the readers, a view into a precious reality—the minds, the hearts, and the souls of these women who graciously invited all of us into their lives. Each woman has bestowed upon us a valuable gift—her story in her words, a glimpse into life in her shoes.

CHAPTER ONE

BALANCING ACT

It's impossible for women to have it all, if they have to do it all. It is ridiculous! We tried to kill [that saying] off for years. It blames the person instead of the structure.

Gloria Steinem, writer, feminist, and social activist

Angela Bovill
Age 40
Interviewed on October 11, 2013 by Christina DeSario
and Amy Williamson of Assumption College
Overseen by Profs. Leslie Choquette and Allison Meyer,
Assumption College

I had a scholarship for the ROTC [Reserve Officers' Training Corps] at University of San Francisco, and I went to school and discovered soon after I got there that this was not what I was called to do. Now, if you have no faith background, you may not understand what I mean by "called to do," but there's something to do with what your life purpose is supposed to be, and I knew that early on, and I knew that's not where I was supposed to be, although I wasn't sure where that was. I just knew it wasn't there, so I gave up my scholarship, which sounds really ridiculous in retrospect, but it turned out well.

I gave it up and went home. I met a person who became my husband not long after that, in the fall after my senior year. I graduated from high school, and I was pregnant by the end of that year. Also not the recommended path. And he already had a son, so at 18 years old, I found myself pregnant with and becoming a mom to an already—well, he was one at the time—child. I was supposed to be that kid that, you know, the most likely to succeed, the one that was going to go on to college, and change the world, and do all these things, and here you find yourself at 18 going [gasp] OK! We're going to plan B! [Laughs] And plan B was not welfare, and it was not all the social programs that were out there to try to make somebody like me survive. It was figure it out, do it anyway, and defy all the odds that happened to be stacked in front of you, and figure out how to make a life for your kids and family.

So, in some sense I know what it means to overcome a lot. I got a job when I was 18 that turned out really good, and I worked really hard, so I got moved up very quickly. I ended up going to college at night, and on the weekends, and wherever I could jam it in on top of being a mother and on top of working full time, and ended up getting my degree in economics and political science. I was working, and working, and working, and working, and I went back for my MBA [Master of Business Administration] at Boston University after that. Thankfully, my employer paid for all that. As long as you can survive the how do you have a job that travels all the time, and you're in school all the time, and you're a full-time mom of three kids at the time—four by the time I took my MBA. You figure out how to survive.

I was in for-profit [business] for about 17 years, traveling around the world. I did mergers and acquisitions. I worked in Europe for about a week a month for about a year. I worked in the Far East for a while, so I've been all over the place. I've had some interesting opportunities, but you wake up kind of at some point in life and you say, "Hmm. There must be a reason why I'm on this planet and it's not necessarily to make this company a lot of money." And so when I left my last company, I left to figure out how to make a difference, and ended up here [Lutheran Social Services of New England] as chief financial officer in 2008. And then, through a series of changes, I ended up as the CEO [chief executive officer] this year.

I guess I can tell you with certainty I'm not the norm in this sector. Most people in the non-profit sector have grown up here. They started here as a social worker. The CEOs in this sector are not my gender. Most of them look like my dad. And I'm not trying to be flip about that, but I was just at a CEO conference a week or two ago, and I walked in the room and I thought, "Oh, good heavens, where am I?" I stick out like a sore thumb. No matter where you see me in any of the conferences, I stick out like a sore thumb. There are lots of women who work in nonprofits, but typically they do more of the direct service work, or human resources, or the other, quote typical female-type jobs. You don't see them at the top of the organizations all that frequently.

I've come to accept who I am and what my role is. I think for the longest time I thought I can be everything to everybody. You're just supposed to work, work, work, work, work, work, work, work all the time. I worked at work, I worked at home. I walked through the door and I was doing laundry, and I would do dishes, and I was chasing kids around, and cleaning out backpacks, and doing all the things you would imagine. Running from work to some kind of school event, trying to appear— maybe to myself, maybe to everybody else, I'm not sure— that I could be everything. And I think, over the course of time, you start to figure out, wait a minute. Wait a minute. And it's interesting because if you look at my career, from the point [of] mid MBA, I started gaining more and more and more confidence. My job has gotten enormous. I was managing three or four people, and now we have 1,500 people on our staff, and another 1,000 volunteers. So, there's a direct correlation between gaining confidence and feeling solid about who you are, and letting go of these predisposed notions that you have to be everything to everybody.

I got confident enough to let go of a really crappy marriage, and faced the fact that that was going to be a big risk, but it wasn't a big risk. My kids are awesome, and they're doing fabulously, and my [current] husband is phenomenal, and he's a stay-at-home dad. He was a dispatcher for the police department.

I haven't done anything at the house for a really long time, unless I feel like it. And it's not because it's below me, it's not. I actually like to clean, but I don't have time for it. By the time I get home from work, it's 7:30 or 8:00 at night. We eat, and I run around and do whatever I need to do, and I go to bed and I get up, and I do it again. By the time we get to the weekends, if I do all that, that means I don't hang out with the kids at all. So I've accepted that I don't go to parent-teacher conferences a lot of the times, my husband does it. He brings them to all their doctors' appointments, and eyeglasses' appointments, or dentist appointments, or whatever it is that has to be done. He does that. I used to try to manage all that, [now] I don't. It's probably the best thing I've ever done, getting to the point where [I] understand that I have a role to play, and my role is I'm supposed to provide for my whole family.

So somehow I let go. When I go to work, I let go. If he needs something, he sends me a message. I certainly respond. If there's something critical, I would certainly go, obviously. But when I work, I work. And I think that's a male trait. I think that's something that men figured out many, many, many moons ago. You cannot be everything to everybody at the same time. And if you're going to be amazing, especially if you're going to do a complicated job like this one or anything like this, you're never going to succeed at it. You'll be suboptimal and going to live out exactly what people say about women which is, "Well they're supposed to be moms, they're too distracted, they're too emotional, and they can't do these jobs." *Yes* you can, but you have to be willing to accept that *no* you can't be a stay-at-home mom, *and* be a CEO of an organization, ain't happenin'. Not and do both well. What it really means is, you'll do both really crummy, and you'll end up really tired, and having nothing left by the end of it.

I think the roles that we choose to play, whether it's being an at-home mom, or working in an organization like this one, or wherever you choose to be, you have to separate the self-worth that you get by being a person of worth just because you're alive, not because of the job you do. Unfortunately, I think a lot of women haven't sorted that out.

I believe women can do *anything* they set their minds to. And hopefully, I'm living proof of that. But I think that they can also be successfully married and have successful kids, too. But you have to come to accept that the rules have changed, and that your rules have shifted, and that it's OK to let go. It's OK to be grateful; it's OK to need somebody else for a different reason. You don't have to be everything.

Renee King
Age 25
Interviewed on November 16, 2014
by Cora Derocher and Michelle
Ruiz of Assumption College
Overseen by Profs. Leslie
Choquette and Christine Keating,
Assumption College

I grew up in Millbury, [Massachusetts], and then I went to Worcester State [University]. I originally thought I wanted to be a teacher. When I was taking my classes and I was doing my student teaching, I realized it just wasn't for me. So I have a degree in psychology, and then when I graduated, I said, "What do I want to do with psychology?" And I didn't really want to go back to school right away. I wasn't really sure what my options were, what I could do. And those were some challenges for me and then being a full-time student and commuting and having to work and I also coach basketball. That's difficult, too, because you take five classes, you work 20 hours a week, you coach. That can make it difficult, too. But I made it through, I graduated [laughs].

[During] my senior year of school I was making cupcakes at home. I would post pictures online on Instagram. And then people would say, "Ohhh my God, can I buy these?" And then all of a sudden, I was making hundreds of cupcakes a week, so about the end of my senior year, I didn't have a job lined up or anything. And this building actually was vacant and for rent, so my parents and I met with the landlords. And we just decided I was going to open a cupcake shop. On a whim. It's worked so far [laughs].

I own [The Queen's Cups.] So I do all the baking and everything else here. For me it's a lot more than the cupcakes. I think it's awesome that I believed in myself and went for something because a lot of people get scared. I was definitely scared, and I had no idea what I was doing. And even now, two years later, I sometimes feel like I don't know what I'm doing. But to be 25 and work for myself, and run a successful business, that means the world to me. And it's also awesome because I have young girls who work for me. And I coach basketball, so I'm connected to these younger girls who want a role model to look up to. I have a lot of people who come in and say, "I read your story, I follow your story, I see your Instagram and it's so cool, but I love to bake at home. And I really want to do what you do. And you just went for it." So that's meaningful, too.

It's definitely difficult [to balance priorities] because when you own a business, that's obviously your first concern always. I work 75 hours a week, sometimes more, especially with the holidays coming up. So it's difficult and, especially in the beginning, I just tried to do everything myself. And you can't do that; you're only one person. And I just was unhealthy. I wouldn't eat or just eat really late at night. And I wasn't taking care of myself and I was miserable. Now I just try to really make sure that I find something for myself every day. Whether it's yoga, or Pilates, or something, just to clear my mind. Because it can be consuming, you know, people are always contacting you, or you're working. And there's not a lot of time for yourself. I think as time has gone on, I definitely have tried to focus on having some time for myself, and making sure every day I do something that I enjoy. You can work all you want, but if you're not happy as a person you're not going to do well at your job.

I don't have any regrets. I think I've made the right moves. I think being young when you're first in college, and you're 18 to 21, all your friends want to go out. Everyone wants to go out and party on the weekends and stuff. And that was something that I missed out on because I was always up early to coach basketball, and now I'm up early to work. And I kind of missed out on some of the fun that my friends had, but I just try to look toward the future, and work hard now, and vacation later, so I think I made the right moves. And I think that when people think of me in 10 years from now, 20 years from now, they'll respect me and what I've done, so I don't really have any regrets.

I don't really have the time to volunteer myself necessarily, but we definitely do a lot of work with the community. I sponsor every sports team in Millbury:

basketball, baseball, tee-ball, and soccer. And I also sponsor the East Side Babe Ruth team in Worcester and we donate a lot. Especially around the holidays I donate whatever cupcakes we have leftover. I donate them to Worcester shelters; sometimes I drop them off at the hospital. We've donated a lot, especially with the Boston Marathon bombings. When it took place, we donated over $2,300. So I wish I had more time to volunteer, I think eventually I will, but I work too much, but [laughs] we definitely try and stay involved for sure. Because it works both ways. It makes us feel good and a lot of people come in from it, too. And sometimes I'll just leave a six-pack of cupcakes outside the door and just say whoever gets here first, it's yours for free, as long as you pay it forward and do something good for someone else. I think that was something that I really wanted to do from the beginning. I wanted to make sure I gave back because that makes a difference. You can make all the money in the world, but if you don't do anything with it, anything positive, there are only so many clothes and things that you can buy. When you do something for someone else, it just makes you feel so much better. So I think as time goes on, [I] will definitely be more involved and be able to volunteer, but for now we just donate.

My parents have done so much for me and they helped me start my business and they have their own full-time jobs, and they come and work here. And they have to deal with my stress more than anyone else, especially around the holidays when I'm mega grouchy, and stressed to the limit. So what keeps me going is knowing that if I keep working hard, I'll be able to do something for them. Like this is their retirement plan and I don't want to put my parents in a nursing home when I am older. I'd like to be able to do something better for them—not better, that's not the right thing to say, but I'd like to take care of my parents and make sure that they are set, that they can retire and not have to worry about it.

When you're younger you kind of have this vision of, "Oh my God, I just want to be rich, have all these things, and have this huge house." And I probably thought the same way when I was younger, but now it is just so much more than that. It's like what you're able to do for people, and providing jobs. It changes over time. It may change again. I'm not really sure, but I'm a little timid to say that we're successful yet, but we'll see [laughs].

We were rated five stars from *Worcester Magazine's* Cupcake Tasting. We were voted runner up Best Cupcakes in 2013 and 2014 in *Worcester Magazine's* Readers' poll. The Queen's Cups was featured as a Local Up & Comer by Go Local Worcester. And lastly, we were voted Best Bakery and Best Dessert in the *Millbury/Sutton Chronicle* Readers' Poll in 2014. These things are great and I am so thankful for them, but my best accomplishment thus far is being in business and making my parents proud.

You grow and some years are harder than others. This year has been probably the worst year of my whole life, but it's crazy because personal-life wise it's been the worst year, but business-wise ever since my life started going downhill, my business has done awesome. So I don't know, I guess it has to balance out somewhere right? [Laughs]

Erin Bradbury
Age 41
Interviewed on February 28, 2014 by Viviana Ayala and Justin Mejia of Assumption College
Overseen by Prof. Carl Keyes, Assumption College

I went to a women's college, so I have a single-sex education which I absolutely loved. I think [it] really contributed to my academic success, my willingness to go on to do an advanced degree. I was really pushed academically. I don't know if I would have gone on to law school if I had some other sort of experience. My major was in government. My minor was in music performance. I would have made it a major [laughs] if I'd been a better performer [laughs], and if I'd thought I could've made a living at it. But I don't think I had enough innate talent, and I didn't think that I could make a full-time living at it. So law filled that gap.

My mother was a great debater. She was on the debate team in her high school, and she was responsible for making me speak up for myself in a lot of different daily teaching moments. I think that helping people and being good at researching, debating, and presenting arguments, those were skills I think I developed in elementary school and middle school. So, my mom was a great influence on me.

My father was the one who prepared me for college. He, from the time I was in the fourth grade, and he realized that I had skills for academics, took me out— I'm sorry, I'm crying—and purchased a desk for me. And we didn't have a lot of money, but he went out and bought me a brand new desk that I picked out, because being a student was my only job. Excuse me [crying]. He encouraged me to look at Smith College. I wasn't looking at any other single-sex schools, and he asked me to look at Smith College, and took me around to all my college interviews and helped me prepare the tape, my audition tape, for all the schools. He's the one [who] went out and bought the equipment to be able to make a recording. I recorded a Mozart concerto, and I played the flute part. So my father was a huge contributor.

Definitely, negotiation is something that they don't really teach you in law school, and it's a very useful skill, as you might imagine, [laughs] in all kinds of different situations, including in my job and at home. Trying to negotiate with a ten year old about whether to stay up ten more minutes or not, is becoming very useful. So, I learned a lot of negotiation skills at some of my prior jobs that have served me very well. Also, the ability to manage time, that's something you've got to be able to do in your position no matter what you choose later on. And so being accountable for time and to know when to stop working on something or when to stop a conference with a client when it no longer is necessarily useful productive information. Those are a couple of skills I learned at jobs up until this point.

Going into business for yourself as a woman, I think, is more difficult than it is for a man. I think a lot of women feel like they need to work for a government agency, or a firm, or a nonprofit. There's some sort of safety in working for others. But when you work for yourself, you have to be the administrator. You need to pay the taxes. You need to be an employer. You need to order the office supplies, be the office manager, and do all of the marketing and then service your clients, get to court on time. I got to a point in my career where I thought I wasn't going to progress any further in terms of responsibility, and so this was the next logical step. But I think that I hesitated for too long—several years before I made that jump to working for myself. I think mainly because my children were young, health insurance—I was the provider—and aversion to risk, but I'm really glad that I did make the leap and I should've done it years prior to when I did.

[Being a lawyer has] given me so much insight into other people's problems. I started off in my early career doing mostly business litigation and dealing with contracts and things like that. Right now I also work with people with mental health issues. I do work in the juvenile court, representing families who are going through care and protection proceedings where children are taken away temporarily or permanently. It never ceases to amaze me that if I think I have any problems, the problems of some of my clients are way worse in terms of mental health issues, substance abuse, poverty, or just an inability to parent. There are so many problems out there that I see as a lawyer, and I see my role as trying to help people through those issues and to counsel them through those issues. So, I mean, whenever I think I've got problems, I just think about some of my clients who may be committed in a state hospital for mental health reasons, or a client whose child was recently taken by the Department of Children and Families who are abused or neglected. I think it's given me a lot of insight into how lucky I am to have my health and my family.

I am part of the Worcester County Bar Association and I chair the Woman Lawyers Committee, which deals with trying to advance women in law, address whatever practice issues that they have, and provide educational opportunities as well. I also co-chair the Juvenile Court Committee for the Bar Association, which deals with, again, juvenile court issues, policies, changes in the law, educational opportunities. I volunteer as a lawyer for a day at Worcester Probate and Family Court once a month, for five or six hours at a time, helping people who can't afford a lawyer to walk them through the process, and fill out their forms, trying to help them navigate the process. I am on the board of the Elder Services of Worcester Area, which helps elders stay at home longer and provide services in their homes. So, I have a lot of volunteer activities, and I hope that I have helped families and individuals and organizations as well. That's very important to me, to give back to the community.

I have a very supportive husband who does a lot of the household tasks right alongside me. He's in charge of laundry [laughs]; I do the cooking, so it's really a modern partnership. So yeah, we share the household responsibilities. Yes, there are some times when I am in trial, where I am just not there. Sometimes weekends, sometimes I have to take phone calls late at night, but I think, for the most part, I am very present for my children and my husband [laughs].

I wish I had more personal time, I would love to

pick up music again, but there are only so many hours in the day [laughs]. But I think overall I have a good balance between work and home. And we do travel quite a bit, and we do a lot of recreational activities as a family. I do wish I had more time for my own personal interests, but I am sure as the children get older I'll have more time later on [laughs]. I think I will try and take lessons again, get back to the point where I was probably at my peak in college, and then play in some sort of community band or orchestra. That would be my dream [laughs]. My dream, when I was in high school, was to be a lawyer and play for the Boston Symphony Orchestra. That didn't exactly pan out, but there's still time.

I mean, my priority right now is taking care of my family—work and community service where I can fit it in [laughs]. I think family life has changed me. It just takes over all of your time. It takes a lot of time, especially trying to raise children nowadays. We really encourage getting outside, skiing, cross-country skiing, biking, hiking, snowshoeing. So family life is the most important aspect, I think in my life right now. And obviously that has changed since before children.

I think that I have a very modern life in terms of balancing advanced degrees and a highly responsible job for other people's lives, with family, with recreation. And women had to fight for so many advances, and I think that I have a very good life in terms of all the opportunities that I have. And I think it's really important to thank the people who came before us for all of those opportunities, because now I don't even have to think about it. I am not someone who's unusual. This is typical life right now, that you can be a lawyer, you can have an advanced degree, you can have a family, you can have a partner who shares the household and childrearing responsibilities with you. So I think that's really important that we've come a long way. I'm sure that there are a lot of other issues that could be improved, but I'm very thankful.

Kerri Melley
Age 40
Interviewed on October 12, 2012 by Kaleigh Hickey and
Matthew Bailey of Assumption College
Overseen by Profs. Leslie Choquette and Esteban
Loustaunau, Assumption College

I couldn't have told you 10 years ago that I
wanted to be a financial advisor. I wanted a school that
had a strong dance program, and a strong liberal arts
education. I studied psychology-based human relations
which was a weaving of psychology, sociology, and child
development. I can certainly say that is something I use in
everything that I do. When I left CC [Connecticut
College], the first 10 years of my life, I expected to
eventually run an arts organization. So that was the path I
was first on.

I danced with several companies in Boston. After
I graduated college, I was working in the administrative
capacity in different arts organizations, and I eventually
ended up working primarily in development with the
fundraising area. So I sort of grew in that career field. I
worked at the BSO [Boston Symphony Orchestra], and
then I took a break from work for a while and went back
and got my MBA [Master of Business Administration]—
again, just sort of hoarding my business skills in the hope
that I would eventually run an arts organization. The last
role I had, I was working at the Easton School of Music
and I was the director of major gifts and planned giving, so
[I dealt with] individuals who are giving to the institution
through life insurance gifts and annuities. I was at a
conference about that topic, and I realized that because I
had my MBA, I understood the financial concepts to a
greater extent than most of the development professionals
who were in the room. Simultaneously, a colleague of
mine who I had worked with and who I had a lot of
respect for—we both shared a background of being artistic

and both had our MBA—he had transitioned out of development and into financial planning. So that is how I got introduced to the field. Ultimately, I made the transition. It is still using a lot of the same skills in terms of building relationships with clients, like I had been using with donors, but again just a different environment. That is how I ended up doing what I do now.

My firm is called Baystate Financial Services and we are a New England financial firm, but as financial planners, we really have our own practices within the greater organization. And I am currently working on building collaboration with two other women financial planners. One works in Beverly [MA] and one works in North Andover [MA]. Because women certainly are a minority in our field and women in general tend to be less educated about their finances and are so busy running the family—many are now working full time or running companies—that we are really dedicated to educating women and empowering women to have better control over their finances. So, that is something the three of us have just started working on. But really, we sort of designed our own practices within the larger firm.

It is really hard being a full-time working mom. And it just gets to the point where you have to be OK not finishing everything, which is hard for me because I was the type of person that everything had to be organized, completed, done perfectly, but you just don't have the time anymore. Also with the work that I do, it is not a traditional 9 to 5 job either. I make my own hours; I meet clients sometimes on the weekends, and sometimes in the evening. So it is a matter of your time and this is my family time, this is my work time, and being able to respect your own time, because everyone will take advantage of your time, if you let them. So it is a matter of just deciding what is important and taking the time for each of those priorities.

I am very lucky, because my husband is a musician. He doesn't work 9 to 5. During the school year he is teaching starting at 2:30. He is home during the day. He takes my daughter to preschool and picks her up. He does the grocery shopping. He does a lot, because he is around during the day, which is great. But I still manage it all, make sure it gets done, coordinate the schedules, and coordinate the childcare. What I will say, my husband is the cook. If I never have to cook again, that would be just fine with me [laughs], so I am very lucky he is a great cook.

I would say that women today have so many more choices. I remember my mom will talk about the fact that, as a woman, when she was growing up, you either went into nursing or teaching. I refer often to a comment that my son made. He was about four or five during the last presidential race and he looked at me and said, "Mom, are you going to be president someday?" And I said, "No, that isn't really the career path that I'm on." "Alright then maybe Sarah will be president." Now, this is his baby sister. So clearly he wasn't going to be president because he has already decided he is going to be a Red Sox player who delivers pizza on his days off. So, he has determined that. But to him it was, "Well, oh OK, then maybe Sarah will be president." It never occurred to me that he probably doesn't even know there has never been a woman president.

Working full time, being a mom, and having a family is a choice you make, and I wouldn't ever make any other choice. But it is a matter, I think, of just finding balance. I don't know, I would say there is a cost to it. I guess I have less time for myself, but that's OK right now. You'll get it back, you'll get it back.

Patricia Eppinger
Age 46
Interviewed on November 11, 2008 by Eliza Cassella and Elizabeth McCarthy of Assumption College
Overseen by Profs. Regina Edmonds and Maryanne Leone, Assumption College

All of my early years including high school were in Northern Virginia. I went to [the College of] William and Mary. I was an economics and government major there, and then went to graduate school at Dartmouth [College], the Tuck School of Business, and got my MBA [Master of Business Administration] there. I'm a graduate school professor, so sometimes I teach executive [education], sometimes I'll teach a semester course. I'm not teaching right now. I mostly teach at Dartmouth, which is why I'm not teaching right now, because the commute is [laughs] three hours each way. I have taught at the Sloan School at MIT [Massachusetts Institute of Technology] as well when we lived in Boston. I truly enjoy it.

When I finished graduate school, I went into consulting, and that was an interesting experience as a woman, just because there are fewer women that go into that kind of work, and the other reason is because a lot of your clients are men. So from '86 until about '97 or so, I was actually working in general management consulting. Most of that time was with a large consulting firm called McKinsey & Company—it's a worldwide firm. And it was great, but a small-ish percentage of women in that environment, though the women were great mentors. And I think that really helped me a lot because you're on the road all the time, long hours and I was working a lot of that time in the South where most of the executives in business were males. So that created some challenges in itself. On the graduate school teaching level, I have had wonderful women I've worked with and that's been a really nice environment.

[Laughs] So who does most of the work around the house do you think, Lou? [Asking her daughter] I think there have been times in our careers where my husband and I have made trade-offs. The first time I actually took a full-time job teaching at Dartmouth at Tuck, we were living in Atlanta. So, that was huge! And it was a big deal, he was traveling for work, and he would accommodate me by flying to New Hampshire rather than flying back to Atlanta. That was pre-kids, but we, at different times in our careers, made those kinds of accommodations. At this point, because of my husband's work, it is pretty much my accommodation. I'm the one, so I've got primary responsibility for these guys [laughs].

When I was younger, particularly out of college and out of graduate school, I was so focused on work; I mean that was just it. And we didn't have kids. I would work around the clock. There were days I'd be working 17, 18 hours a day. And it was just because I thought that's what it took [laughs]. And I thought that that's what I wanted to be doing, and then as I got a little bit more senior in my work, I was able to mentor some younger folks. When I was in Atlanta, I was the president of the board of the YWCA, and I got a sense that there were other priorities in life. If I wanted to I could stay at work all the time, and I would never get it all done. Right? And so at that point, I had to say what's important and getting that other side of life, of just doing something that's important to the community, maybe to further a mission or a goal that you believe in. So that shaped a lot of what I do now. I like working, when I'm working, but I also know that there are other parts of my life that are important.

I do a lot of community work here with boards in Worcester and in Grafton, kids' school, that kind of thing.

And I hope that for my own daughters I would be a role model, in terms of doing a little of everything. Not doing it all and not doing it all perfectly, but they know that when I am doing work, that we do have to bring in extra support to get them to and from school, but they know that the work is important. I am going to be the incoming chair of the board of the EcoTarium and my kids refer to that as the place I work, because I like to spend a lot of time there. But what I do now, I guess, is I try to choose things that are important to my family, too. So, I do the EcoTarium work, I'm on the board of their school, on the vet school [Tufts University School of Veterinary Medicine] here in Grafton just because animals, and kids, the family are really important to me. But there are so many wonderful things in Worcester that you can be involved in, and one of the things I really like is this network of women that exists in Worcester which I haven't necessarily found in other cities.

My husband and I have both always been big supporters of the United Way. And as needs change and as ways that people give to different charities change, we've always felt like there's some need for an organization like that. So for 20 years, we've been involved with the United Way. I was happy to see there was a Women's Initiative here, when we moved here, because we had been involved in one in Atlanta. The organization's great because they let you be involved in ways that fit your life, and right now I can't be at everything. I can't necessarily even be on a committee, just because a lot of committees meet in the evening, which is harder to do. So they let me be involved in a way that I can be, which is to be a great cheerleader for the organization, to help other people in the selection of their priorities. I am going onto an advisory committee that they have now—they're very creative. The meetings are once a month but sometimes, some months they're at 8:45 which is great after I drop my kids off at school, or they're at noon for people who can do stuff during the lunch hour. And so it fits. You feel like you can make a difference, you can be involved. Great women are involved. I'm excited about the focus on adolescent girls, as my daughter is coming into that age. It's a challenge whether you're from an affluent situation or not. I think it's great how they've mobilized women in the community. I'm just really impressed!

I think success in my life is the balance, is spending enough time with my kids so that they feel like they see their mom and they see their parents. It's contributing to the community, whether it's our church, their school, the Women's Initiative, the EcoTarium. And it's having some meaningful work. I do a lot of writing and particularly when I was younger, I used to write in business journals, and that's the kind of thing I can do anytime. And so, I feel like I have my hand in it. I was just doing some training for two professors at Dartmouth who were taking over a course that I did, and I was on the phone with them a lot.

They used to say, "You can have it all," women and the glass ceiling, and all that kind of stuff. I think women can do whatever they want to do—I do. But I also think, like anyone else in their own lives, you have to make trade-offs. My husband would probably, I know he'd love to be spending more time with the kids, he'd love to be a basketball coach [laughs]. But right now, this is what he's doing and it's the right thing for our family. For me, a little more mom time would be good [laughs]. You know? But I like that I can, whether it's writing or teaching, I can do something in that arena. I keep my brain active by doing the not-for-profit kind of work. I'm excited to spend time with [my children].

Laura Caswell
Age 50
Interviewed on May 2, 2011 by
Fitore Gjemnica and Audrey
Hazel of Assumption College
Overseen by Prof. Carl Keyes,
Assumption College

I think everybody feels like they have to work. I think there are a lot of women who still would like to stay home and raise their kids. I think there's still an undercurrent of that in the culture that you'll graduate college, you'll work, you'll get married, and then you take some time off and raise your kids. I don't even know if that's wrong, and I don't know if it means we necessarily changed. Because on some level I think—and, you know, nature, nurture, culture, blah, blah, blah [laughs]. I think a lot of women still want to have kids, you know what I mean? Men and women still want to get married and raise a family, and so how do you balance all that? I think it's easier for women who don't want to. My sister has been married for 26 years and doesn't have kids, and some people wonder about that, but it's not—she's not looked at as a weirdo. It's not like, "Hmm, you never had kids." But I think there's still an expectation that that's what women will do, and I think you have to fight it a little bit when you don't. My sons have joked about staying home and being stay-at-home dads [laughs]. I think that's even a harder trend than for a woman to step back and say, "I'm going to take some time off and raise my kids." I think it's harder for a woman to say, "I'm going to work, and my husband is going to stay home and take care of the kids." I think what happens is both people in a marriage work, and the kids go to daycare. I don't want that to sound like I think it's an evil thing, but that idea of a man staying home and raising the kids is still not the norm in our society [laughs].

Part of my decision [to stay at home] really was that I got married at the end of my freshman year in college, so I hadn't finished school. My ex-husband—my husband at the time—had graduated. He's a computer programmer, and so he had some pretty good jobs that enabled me to stay home. We both wanted me to finish school. We made some sacrifices that way because the types of jobs that I probably would have gotten would have been minimum wage jobs without the education, but I enjoyed it. I mean staying home with two year olds can be mind numbing at times, but I don't regret any of it. Going to work when I got divorced was tough in some ways, because I hadn't worked and juggling the kids and everything. Career wise, salary wise, I got a late start and didn't start working until I was 37, so I started at a low end of the pay scale. I didn't have the experience, and in some ways I won't work long enough because I'm working for the state and education, I don't get paid as much. But if I did a private sector thing I would never catch up, because I hadn't worked for 15 years, but I don't regret any of it. One of the things I've always known about myself is that I did want to grow up and be a mommy. I had a tough time when the kids left because I felt, "The only job [I] wanted is gone." [Laughs] The only job I wanted, even graduating high school and knowing I could be a doctor, a lawyer, a banker or whatever. Everything for me was go to college, get married, have kids, and everything else was secondary for me. That's what I always wanted to do is raise a family, so I've been lucky that I've been able to do it. I know a lot of women who have to work in jobs they don't want to do in order to put food on the table. It's one thing if you've got a job that you enjoy or that you want to do, but just to work to make ends meet is tough.

I have the degree in computer science and my former professor let me know about [the job], and at the time it was a part-time position. I applied and came on the interview and then I didn't get the job and they hired somebody else. A month later they called me up and the person who had taken the job said she didn't want it, so I was second choice [laughs]. [The] first two and a half years were part time and then it became a full-time position. In one respect, being able to work part time for a while meant I could have the time I needed to be with my kids which was great. And then, being able to get full time when I was ready for it, was fantastic.

When I was a stay-at-home mom, I did all of [the housework] and that was partly my choice. Because I was home, it seemed silly for my ex-husband to work a 40 to 50 hour workweek, and then come home and do a load of laundry. Then I started working and got divorced; I hired a cleaning lady and [laughs] I still have my cleaning lady even though nobody's at home anymore. Every once in a while [I think] I should get rid of her because I really don't need a cleaning lady [laughs]. I'm not that messy, but I enjoy it and my cleaning lady is a single mom herself. She's about my age, and her kids are grown, too. I know she can use the work—I mean it's not just pity; it's really selfish [laughs]. I don't clean my own toilets, [laughs] so I keep her. I haven't done that in like 15 years. I just don't want to go back to that [laughs].

[How have I balanced different priorities in my life?] I was just saying to my girlfriend this afternoon, "Not very well." [Laughs] My father is a workaholic and my sister, brother, and I have sort of picked up that tendency from him. The job that I do is problem solving. I don't intend [to] go home and think about it, but things will come to me. And so sometimes I'll make myself a note, and other times I'll actually log on and do it, and work after hours. So, I don't let go of my work probably as much as I should. Other weekends I'll go home, and I'll be fine. So it varies, but sometimes I think I get a little obsessive with that kind of stuff. I need to balance a little bit better, but I do know when it gets out of whack, because I get cranky [laughs]. I start thinking I am the most put-upon person on the face of the earth, nobody has to do as much work as I do; nobody, nobody, has it as bad as I do. And as soon as I start feeling like that, I just know I'm being cranky, so usually I stay away, so I don't make everybody throw a pity party for me, but [laughs] I just do something to relax and—this is ridiculous—feel sorry for a couple of hours, and then I do something fun, and then I'm usually over it [laughs]. Everybody deserves to throw their own little pity party. It's just you don't have to inflict it on the whole world [laughs]. I'm chilling out; I'm not talking to anybody [laughs].

Barbara Guertin
Age 53
Interviewed on April 3, 2014 by
Olivia Bowie and Carolina
Santos of Assumption College
Overseen by Prof. Carl Keyes,
Assumption College

I am a professional actor. Started acting in New York City at 12 years old. I am a member of all the acting unions for several decades now. I moved here in 1998, but I started coming here back in 1990 when I was asked to audition for a play at Foothills Theater. I met my husband, I think it was 1995. We dated for three years and then decided that we'd get married. All in one year I moved, got married, and had a baby because I had my daughter the last day [laughs]. She came a couple of weeks early, so I fit it all in [laughs]. Oh, I did get the play, the first one and I subsequently did seven shows at Foothills Theater.

Since I've been in Worcester for 15 years, I've gotten the opportunity to work for a couple of different industries. And in those industries, insurance, health insurance, I've been in biotech, medical devices, genetic testing, and medical equipment. In Worcester, obviously being here for 15 years I've seen a large change, and just working for Fallon [Community Health Plan] for the last two years, I've seen a significant increase in some of the leadership roles now being populated by women. So I do have to say I see it on the rise. I'd love to see a women sitting as city manager now that we're looking again for a city manager. Wouldn't that be interesting, especially—I don't want to say it's been an old boys' network here, but it has been an old boys' network here.

Yes, I did [want to go to graduate school]. I was the last person cut actually from Yale Drama [laughs]. It was between myself and one other person, and that sort of was my dream to go to Yale Drama and once that didn't pan out, I just thought I will just work. I'll work in theater and so forth. Granted, I always had a day job. I always tried to find day jobs that were flexible and that's how I got into recruitment because even until today, I'm still a working actor. I may work here and I have a very serious position here, but I do have time off and I will take time and I will get calls to do parts or extra work or something on a movie set, and I will absolutely do it [laughs]. Just because it's a change of scenery and even though I am technically working, I'm taking a vacation day to work. I enjoy that so much, the change of scenery; I learn something every time I do that. So last year, I took about five days. I shot an online brokerage video for Fidelity, and I got to work within a scene with *American Hustle*, and worked on it actually two days.

Well, [laughs] depending on who you would ask, I don't know whether balance should be that phrase, but first of all family comes first. It does and I think sometimes people see my pictures in the papers and magazines and so forth, "Oh she's out and about all the time." There's no way I could be. I've got two kids, and they're very high maintenance [laughs] and I'm with them.

I'm basically home cooking dinner every single night, which is not standard. I think a lot of working women don't do that. Cooking is one of my creative outlets, so I enjoy it. It also helps me maintain their weight and their nutritional guidelines, and I make home-cooked meals. I don't do a lot of out of a bag or a box or something, so I think it's important that any parent is cognizant about that. And I do try to be a part of their schooling. They're now in sixth and ninth grade. But you can't do it all for them, they have to do a lot for themselves, too. And I never think anyone would call me a helicopter mom, however, I've been told that I'm more involved with their health and well-being than a lot of parents are. So to me, that's the best compliment, but it's not like it's overly obvious. I'm not one of the parents beating down the school doors, [laughs] "I need to be in that classroom watching over my Johnny," or something. I've never done that. When [they were] in the earlier grades I was definitely one of the moms who always went on the field trips. I was always reading [to them] up until fourth grade. You can go in there once a week and read to the kids which I obviously loved to do because I love stories. I love being animated and teaching because that is something that I've always enjoyed. I think anyone who directs and produces is really a teacher at heart, that's why you're doing it. You're facilitating others to do what you know in your brain. For actors or set designers, anything, you're teaching them, "How about the vision?" and helping them facilitate.

I've gotten smart in the last couple of years, and I've invested in more than I should probably in some family vacations. You work so hard, and my husband works just as hard as I do. He is a rock and roll drummer, so we're both very creative. We have our yin and yang sides, and I just basically said, "We're going away!" So the last couple of years we've gone on weeklong vacations, which is new for us. We hadn't gone on one since 2005, and I think it really brings a family closer. I think when you have a whole family unit together with no distractions, it just makes us all work better as an entity, but you know the cost, the cost is great.

[How do I identify myself as a woman living in Worcester?] That's a great question. Well it all depends on the audience, [when] somebody asks me who I am. If I'm at a children's function, I'm Alexis's and Max's mom, and if I'm at some type of business function, I'm probably from Fallon Health [laughs]. If I'm with the film industry folks, I'm an actress, producer, director. I think it really depends on the audience, but in general I like to think of myself as someone who's trying to make a difference here in Worcester. Someone who's trying to create more jobs, redirect people to the right ones, open up avenues for economic growth for the city that have not formerly been there. Such as building a film studio, which is one of my projects, additionally, starting a new theater company, and hiring actors for events all over the city for all of the different cultural institutions.

Katherine Mangsen
Age 47
Interviewed on March 26, 2012
by Laura Kuchar and Terri
Whelan of Assumption College
Overseen by Prof. Carl Keyes,
Assumption College

        It used to be very
strange to have a woman funeral director, but now people tend to prefer, at least in this practice, to deal with women. I graduated from [College of the] Holy Cross in 1986, then I got married, and then I started having a family. So I had all of the kids before I went back to work. I call it my second career, being a mom was my first career. Once I had the experience of being a mom and got a little older, I

went back to school to Mount Ida College and got my funeral directing degree. And now I feel a lot more welcome in the business world, and I don't know if it is my maturity, my age, my experience, my career path that I chose, but back then I didn't feel like I had as many opportunities as I have now. But I just wanted to be a mom at that point.

[How do I balance responsibilities?] I ask for a lot of help! My older daughter helps. My oldest is 24, then I have a 21-year-old, a 16-year-old, a 13-year-old, and an 11-year-old. So the older kids help with the younger kids, and my husband has been a funeral director for over 30 years. So we kind of flip-flopped jobs. I was at home and, until I went back to school, I had the kids. And he was working here. Then I went back to school, and now he's at home. He does work a little bit, but I love being out here and working.

I would say the professional [costs], as far as dealing with death and dealing with grief and grieving people, it's tiring. At the end of a really big funeral, it's emotionally exhausting to see people sad all the time. But the more I do it, the more I can almost remove myself from it. When I first started, if somebody was crying, I'd be crying with them. But then you realize that you need to be their support, because you're there for them, you're directing them, and you are leading them with the process. So with the more experience I got, and after being schooled, I realized, "Yes, you want to cry, but you need to be strong." It's like a ministry or a calling. And I would say that my kids do have to understand that we can get called out day and night, holidays, weekends, there are no times that death doesn't happen. And they're just really understanding because they don't know anything else. What we told them, too, is that the person whose loved one passed away isn't coming back, but we'll be back in a couple hours.

I consider it like a ministry to help serve people

through the worst times of their lives. My dad passed away suddenly when I was 11, and it was a horrible experience being an only child, and it was my first experience with death. And I don't want anyone else to go through what I did, so I want to make it better for them. So, I took a negative experience, and I'm trying to make it positive for people, make it comforting here when they come in. We have a toy section for kids. We know that people don't want to be here. So we try to make it as comforting as possible, instead of the old Lurch at the door, the whole Addams Family [television show] atmosphere of old funeral homes. Forget it. No.

My first degree is a bachelor's from Holy Cross in religious studies and political science. And actually I use my religious studies degree a lot in dealing with different religions, when we deal with burying them. So even though [it was] way back when I got the degree, I'm still using it today. I was brought up Lutheran, went to a Jesuit college, and learned the Catholic traditions. While I was at Holy Cross I learned [about] Islam, Buddhism, Hinduism, and I just think that all traditions should be accepting of other traditions. So just by knowing the other traditions and the pitfalls where one tradition would say, "We're right, you're wrong." No, we all work together. We all believe in a God, some other being. I've even dealt with American Indians where they believe in spirit mother or spirit earth. And you [are] open to all those things, and serve them because death is constant.

Everyone experiences, no matter what religion they are, birth and death. And you can't get away from it. So, the traditions might be different in how you bury your dead and what religious ceremonies you go through burying your dead. [It] doesn't change the feelings you have. We accept which tradition you belong to whether it's Christian or—we don't really do Jewish people. I have learned a lot about the Jewish religion, but they tend keep to their own Jewish funeral homes. But you are still mourning, and you're still human, you still have the same emotions, regardless of your religion.

You can do whatever you want to do, you can have a career, you can have kids, and you can do it all. Everyone is equal, and don't let anyone stand in your way. And, of course, always think outside the box. At Holy Cross that's the big thing. Think outside the box. Don't take no for an answer, always question everything.

Marianne Felice
Age 69
Interviewed on April 4, 2013
by Andrea Burnette and Lorin
Colucci of Assumption
College
Overseen by Prof. Carl Keyes,
Assumption College

My mother died when I was 10 years old. And so I went to Catholic school, and in many ways it was the nuns who really raised me and taught me my set of values, and what was important to me and what wasn't. When I finished high school, I actually entered the convent for a few years. My mother superior thought I would be a very good doctor someday. And she's the one who suggested I go to medical school. That's why, without her, I would never have done this.

I knew I wanted to do pediatrics. I've always known I wanted to work with children, and actually my sub-specialty was adolescent medicine. So I did my pediatric residency and then I had a choice, I could either just go into practice—well presuming I passed and got my license and everything else to practice medicine—or I could go on for more sub-specialty training and teach. Before I went to medical school, I actually taught high school. I loved it, loved teaching teenagers and so when I finished medical school, I ended my pediatric training. Then I took more training as a sub-specialty in adolescent medicine, where I cared for pregnant teenagers, anorexia nervosa, kids who were depressed, kids on drugs, all this stuff with teenagers, sexually transmitted diseases, etc.

And so, I did think about my options, but for me, I think being with young people was just so important to me, I still do. And I think teaching was so important to me that I knew that I was destined for an academic career, and then from there I just moved up and kept seeing patients, doing research, publishing, until I became a chair myself.

When I went to medical school, only 10 percent of the class could be women. So I'm of that generation where we were fighting for women's rights, and it's hard to explain that even to our young medical students where 50 percent of the class is women, and when I was a medical student they were all guys, well mostly all guys. There were just so few women that we couldn't change the culture of the field until there were enough of us.

The University of Massachusetts Medical School recruited me to come here. In 1998 I was happily working at the University of Maryland Medical School, in Baltimore, and the previous chair of pediatrics here at UMass stepped down, and they had a search committee, which is common, looking for the new chair. They chose me after I interviewed and visited the campus. My husband and I moved to the Worcester area. We live in Shrewsbury and I began my job as the chair—the job I had until two months ago—as the chair of pediatrics at the University of Massachusetts Medical School. I was the only woman chair here for over 10 years.

I really wanted to take care of kids and influence the lives of children, and that's by teaching other doctors to take care of them, and it's also by publishing and doing research as to what helps. Then you get to be known nationally. You are asked to speak everywhere, you're given grants, and invited to be on panels. So as you get to be known more, your leadership abilities get noticed by people and so, at some point, I had to decide. Am I willing to be a leader in the field, which is a lot more responsibility on your shoulders, or not? Well, I like being in charge. I like being organized and saying, "Let's do it like this, let's try to do that." When you're in that position, you also can have an influence on the younger physicians below you, you can guide them, you can facilitate their growth so that they can have an impact and that's sort of what led me to do that.

[What has this work meant to me?] Just everything. It's meant that I can put my stamp on Central Massachusetts, and in building a program for children's health. Before I arrived here, the department was only half the size it is now and we were accredited to be a children's hospital. I guess I recruited over 100 faculty to come and join us in PEDS [Pediatrics]. And we've been able to have influence in the whole community, so many of our faculty are out on the boards. I was United Way, Girls Inc., YWCA. I'm losing track of all the different organizations in Worcester that we could have influence on that helped children. And that's what it has meant to me. Particularly not having my own children, I think I just decided that all the children in Central Massachusetts are all my children, and that I can have an influence on what happens to them.

I don't know if I never managed to have children because of the stress of the job. I mean we certainly were evaluated, and we certainly tried. I don't know if that is one reason why I didn't have children, or if God knew I wasn't going to have children and said, "I want you to use your talents to take care of other people's children." I don't know that, but in the back of my head, I sometimes think about that. Why couldn't I have had any? You know, why didn't I have any?

When I was chair, I was maybe putting in 70-hour workweeks, so it's hard to take care of your house and do everything at the same time. And I often did my emails from 10:00 p.m. to 2:00 a.m., so it was very hard to do everything. So I hire somebody to clean the house, and I fire them if they don't clean it as well as I do [laughs]. But there are still some things that I still do. I still like to do my own grocery shopping. I still like to do my own personal laundry. I actually love to iron, there's something so relaxing to me, and the reason is you iron it, and fold it, and it's done. The rest of my work I do it, and it's still not done. When you iron something it's done, and I have a sense of accomplishment like I've actually done something. I like gardening. So even though there's a man who takes care of our yard overall, there's a patch of flowers that I get. They're mine so if they need to be weeded, I do them. So again, weeding is you actually do it, and it finishes. You know you've got something done. And I think of the department that I ran as a garden. I think of all the faculty that I've recruited as a flower. I could have had all roses, you know, real flashy but they have thorns, roses do. Or you can have all tulips, but I think of the faculty in the department as different kinds of flowers. Some need lots of sunshine, some need lots of water, some are going to be OK with benign neglect, they don't even need you.

Poorly. That's how I've done [balance]. Just poorly. I don't know how to do that balance. I hope your generation figures out how to do it. When you're a woman who's the only woman of 10, you can't fail. The women of my generation in medicine felt we had to be better than men to justify the fact that we had a place to sit at that table. And I don't think that men put it on us; I think we put that on our shoulders. I have trouble balancing; I also have this stupid idea that I have to do everything perfectly. So it's bad enough that I don't even balance it, but then I do it so that it would be perfect, which is stupid. So I don't do well at balancing. But my husband and I try to have a date night once a week. Our idea of a date was watching Netflix and having a bottle of wine. That was about it, but at least we would be spending some time together. I've tried to remember to do things outside of medicine. I love reading novels. I read a lot. I play tennis, and a couple years ago I took up the drums. When I was a little girl, I tap danced.

[My advice to women?] Go for it girl! Go for it! You can do anything you want to do, and don't let anybody hold you back! That's what I would tell the women of today. And the next thing I would say is figure out how to balance, because I never figured it out.

Tanja Olson
Age 75
Interviewed on March 11, 2014
by Jason Duke of Assumption
College
Overseen by Prof. Rachel
Ramsey, Assumption College

My parents were both from Germany. They, in 1939, left Germany due to the Second World War, and Hitler, and his German Jewish—I am trying to think of the word—it wasn't then called the Holocaust, but the treatment of the German Jews and the fear that they would not survive the war. They decided to leave Germany at that point. I was six months old, and they managed to get a ship from Hamburg, Germany, to Shanghai, China. In 1940, my grandmother, Margaret Mendel, my mother's mother joined us. And she was not Jewish. My grandmother lived in Germany, was born in Germany. She married a Jewish man that caused a little problem in her family. And she later moved to Berlin. She had one daughter, and the daughter was my mother.

Children have a different way of looking at things, so as far as I was concerned [Shanghai] was my home. My father had opened a pharmacy when we first came from Germany, and due to the Japanese invasion over in China, he had to close the pharmacy. The Japanese were—I can't think of the word—were in league with, I guess, the Germans. So they decided to intern all the German Jews, so my family, my mother, father and I, were interned in a school and we had a half of a room, which was a small room. It was not a big room, and we stayed there until after the end of the war. My father died shortly after we were there, and my mother died just after the end of the war in Asia in 1945. And it was just after it, I think the end of the war was in September, she died in December. My father died when I was almost four years old. He died of cholera. And my mother died when I was seven. So then I ended up living with my grandmother, who took me in.

Like all children, you get very adaptable to whatever your circumstances are and our circumstances were such that even though we didn't have much, and we certainly didn't have a lot of space, it was kind of exciting to live with a lot of other people where there were a lot of children. I went to two different schools while I was there, one was a German Jewish school, and after that closed, I actually ended up in an English Jewish school—a British Jewish school probably would be a better way to put it. And so to me, it was an exciting place to live. I definitely think of it as home rather than any other place. There were several years I didn't go to school at all because that was due to the fact that the Communists came and the schools closed. So I didn't go, and my grandmother didn't want me to be far away because there were bombings and fights in the streets and so forth.

That trip [to the United States] was quite interesting in some ways. I thought it was very exciting being almost 11 years old. We got onto a ship in Shanghai, the SS General Gordon. And we were on third class, so we were not in the greatest of places. We landed in San

Francisco. The trip over was, like I said, interesting because we stopped in two different places. We stopped in Yokohama, Japan, we stopped in Hawaii, and then we landed at San Francisco.

And we went to Worcester due to the fact that some of the churches in the Worcester area were, at that point, getting involved in trying to sponsor people and it was, I think, a Baptist church; the family that decided to sponsor us were here in Worcester. And when we got to San Francisco, we got a ticket on a train and went all the way across the country from San Francisco to Chicago, from Chicago to Worcester.

I did well in school. I would have liked to have gone to college. I did end up having a job once I graduated from high school actually. I got my job before I graduated from high school. Two years before, I started working for Paul Revere [Insurance Company] and part time during high school, so I stayed with that and it was a decent job. And then I ended up getting married—getting engaged and getting married. So I would have liked to have a college education, but I think I have enough lifetime experiences that I don't ever feel that I have missed anything. So I do feel that I am an educated person, probably know more about a lot of things than most college graduates.

My first choice was I became a mother and I stayed home for quite a few years and volunteered. At that point I wasn't living in Worcester, so I volunteered at Holden Hospital. I ran their gift shop, and I went and worked in their emergency room for quite a few years. Enjoyed every minute of it. When my kids grew up and there were family problems, I decided I would take a regular job, and I worked in the surgical intensive care unit of Memorial Hospital in Worcester, and I did enjoy that. I stayed there for about a year and after that I decided I would do something different. I happened to have a friend, who wanted to open a shop, and she and I became partners and we opened a shop in West Boylston. I had that for six years. Gave that up, worked for another friend—she had a curtain shop, and then she was an interior designer—and worked with that. Then [I] decided that I would do something different again and got a job with the bank. Worked with that until I decided to retire, but went back to work part time.

I guess I really never did make up my mind what I wanted to be [laughs]. I just went from thing to thing, and most of the time part time. I was lucky that my husband had a good career, and I didn't have to work. [Working meant] independence. I always felt that from the day I got married, that everything we had as far as money was concerned, was my husband's money. I mean it was ours as a family, and I felt that I should have something of my own. That if I wanted to—if we wanted to go on a trip or I wanted to give a gift to my husband, that I wasn't just taking money from him, and then giving it back to him. So I basically wanted to have money of my own, that I could use for those things so that we could have extras— little extra things that we wanted to do like take a trip, or I bought him a car, or things like that. So, those are the kind of things that I wanted out of the career of doing things on my own, making some money, and it was in—I probably started working in the '80s, maybe in the middle or lower '80s that I started working for money. Other than that, I volunteered before that pretty much.

I guess I never thought of it as giving up anything because I still did the things that I enjoyed. My favorite things to do are still the same as they were then, and that's reading, and theater, and doing things that gave me pleasure. And I was able to do that while my kids were growing up as well as later, but I think what I basically gave up was the feeling that I have now of independence, of being able to do what I want when I want to do it. I had the responsibility of the family, and I wanted to make sure they grew up to be the kind of people that I would like them to be. And we did a lot with my husband's family, and I didn't have any family—obviously, my grandmother died when my children were young. So I really didn't have any family, so it was basically my husband's family that we spent a lot of time with. So I don't think I gave up anything, as such. I made some choices, and I think the choices I made were the right ones. You can always look back and say the what-ifs, but I think, as a woman, I basically did what I felt were the right things to do at the time and I don't regret them.

Kendra Timko-Hochkeppel
Age 39
Interviewed on January 29, 2008 by Tiffany LaRose of College of the Holy Cross
Interpreters: Sarah Bairich and Anna Harris of Northeastern University
Overseen by Prof. Judy Freedman Fask, College of the Holy Cross

I'm 39 years old. I was born deaf. I'm the third generation in my family to be Deaf. I use my voice when I have to, but I prefer not to. My husband's name is Matt and he, too, is Deaf. We have two beautiful girls. The older is two and a half and her name is Carissa. The younger is seven months old and her name is Merna and they both can hear.

[We moved to Worcester] in 2004. My husband and I wanted to buy a house and we searched many places and they were so expensive, and we found that Worcester had affordable houses. So we moved here to Worcester and we like it here. It's close to major highways and it's also close to my parents' house in Connecticut. We feel that Worcester is in the perfect location, you can shoot over to Boston, you can shoot up North, down South. We just really like it here.

We've always had hardships and struggles, but as technology changes, we have more access to things and our lives have improved. So, it's not only Worcester, but America in general. Now we have video phones, we have AOL Instant Messenger, closed captioning, pagers, and cell phones. We can't live without our pagers. Our lives have changed as technology has changed.

Elementary, middle, and high school should have something in their curriculum that teach kids about other types of kids. Or people with disabilities, deaf people, deaf-blind people, people with Usher syndrome, just all different types of people. I worked at the Deaf-Blind Department at Deaf Inc., in Boston, and some of the students who were deaf never heard of a deaf-blind person before. It was crazy. Schools should expand more about different types of people, and the kids just need to be aware.

I grew up in Fairfield, Connecticut, and I went to school there. I went to public elementary school— mainstream, but they had a deaf program there. I was lucky, the teacher that I had for first, second, third, and fourth grade, knew how to sign. So, I was really lucky. I was with "oral" [philosophy]. I knew how to read lips, and talk a little, so we'd go back and forth between that and signing, and I was fine. In fifth grade, it got a little harder. The teacher didn't know sign language, but I could read lips and the teacher would always look at the kids and talk to them. So I was fine. I managed just fine.

When I entered middle school, I had to use an interpreter. The teacher would always talk while writing on the board, and she wouldn't talk to us. I couldn't see her lips to read them, and it was hard because I wasn't used to using an interpreter. And I continued using an interpreter when I was in college. But understand I wasn't the only deaf student there. They had a deaf program. So, I was fine.

I was really lucky. My family was Deaf, so if I

didn't understand something at school, I'd go home and ask my parents. They'd be able to explain everything to me [in American Sign Language- ASL]. So, I had great communication at home. I was really lucky. Some people would go home and their parents didn't know sign language, so they struggled at home and at school. [In school] I had note takers. I had friends who could sign. It was [like] having two schools; regular school and then home school. My parents taught me about life. School won't teach you that.

I went to Northeastern University in Boston and I majored in human services. I began working and went back to college, to Salem State College, for a Master's of Social Work. And I've been working ever since. I've decided I don't want to go back to school. I've had enough.

After I graduated college, I worked at the Massachusetts State Association for the Deaf [MSAD], in their Sign Language Department. I wanted to work with hearing parents [who had] deaf children. I wanted to do that kind of work and I worked there for about four years. Deaf Inc., had a position open for Independent Living Services as the director there, so I applied [and was hired]. It was definitely a challenge, but I really liked that job. When I had my first daughter—that job was a high demand job. My energy was just really consumed from that. I thought that if I worked there and I was also at home with my kids, then my energy would be gone. My daughter was my priority. I discussed it with my husband and I decided to leave Deaf Inc. So, I left, but I really could not completely leave Deaf Inc. That's where my heart was. Deaf Inc., happened to have another position open in the Deaf-Blind Department. I took a job there once a week as the director's assistant. I would do secretarial work like filing, typing letters, and things like that for my supervisor. Unfortunately two weeks ago they let me know that the position I have now won't be needed anymore. Now, my husband and I can focus more on a home business that we have and try to expand that. We'll see. We'll see where this leads us.

Right now, I'm mostly a full-time mom. I don't work with parents or kids right now, and over the years my goals have changed. My husband and I want to be home for our kids. We want to be there for them. We want to watch them grow up. Our kids are our top priority. Your life changes when you have kids.

We own an Internet business. What we do is order things through the Internet, and earn a commission from the products that we order. And we expand the business by involving other people into that. For the business I have now, everything is accessible for the Deaf community. We're really lucky because everything we need for this business is completely accessible. We have DVD with closed captions, workshops with interpreters; everything is accessible for the Deaf and hard-of-hearing with this kind of business.

[How do I balance my priorities?] Well, actually, I have a clone. She's just like me. No, I'm just kidding. Well, I just do it, I just do it. It's in me. Every day I have a routine, and I wake up and follow that routine. My husband and I always communicate about our schedules, so if I have to go out, he has to watch the kids. Like today I [said], "Hey, I'm going out for a few hours," and we agreed on the schedule. It's not like life before when you just wake up, and run out of the house. You need a schedule and a routine. My husband and I have our plan books, and we match them, and coordinate them to make sure we know where the kids are, where both of us are, and it's tough. But if we didn't have those plan books and that schedule, we'd be hopeless. We'd be lost.

But first of all, my priorities, I'm always a mom. Life changes and so now, when we're with our kids, we're looking for places that they can come too. Our friends [who] don't have kids, they go out and [say], "No, the kids can't come," and we just say, "We can't go." We want our kids to be with us wherever we go. They have to allow our kids to join. We don't want our kids home with a babysitter or a friend. I want them to spend the time with us, we're a family. It's hard. Our lives are changing.

No regrets, I was able to do so many things before I got married. I've been married for almost four and a half years now. We got married late, but I absolutely had the opportunity to live my life. I had the opportunity to experience so many things. I got to travel. Not quite as much as my parents do now, but still I got to travel. I was Miss Deaf Connecticut in 1989. I was able to experience so many things with that. It opened so many doors. I met so many people and I got to go to the Miss Deaf America Pageant and meet people there. I got to go to college. I had a lot of fun in college. I feel like I've had enough experiences and I don't regret anything. Now I'm married and I have kids and life is changing, but still absolutely no regrets. New experiences and a new life and it's awesome. I regret nothing.

Jennifer Stanovich
Age 51
Interviewed on
November 17, 2010
by Ethan Ward,
Katherine Vachawski,
and Jordan Sweigart
of Assumption
College
Overseen by Prof.
Arlene Guerrero-Watanabe, Assumption College

I interned at the United Way of Central Mass [Massachusetts]. My task was to put together a booklet. I was in public relations and communications and was a psych [psychology] major, and I had to put together a booklet of media contacts. I mean, nowadays, you would just obviously Google that, but then you needed to have something in front of you. So I put this booklet together and when it came time to apply for jobs, the first place I went to was Thom McAn Shoe Company here in Worcester. They had already seen this booklet because I distributed it throughout the city, and then [I was] hired based on my opportunities here. You've got to take advantage of those things when they come up.

[My] mentor was fabulous, Angela Dorenkamp. She worked very closely with me, and got me into this internship program, and that's what started my career. I am still on the same career path that she put me on. Then once you get into the professional field, it was important to be in some of the groups that are out there. There are a lot of networking groups that exist, and one of the ones that I joined was the Worcester County Editors Council, and it was all people who were editing newsletters like I was, and in communications, and the contacts that I made there led to my next job. So, it's definitely a lot of who you know.

While I was at Thom McAn, that was when computers were just coming out. Word was that computers were the thing of the future and this is the way to go. I had contacts from the Worcester County Editors Council and one of the guys that I knew there said, "I'm at Data General," [which] was one of the big computer companies at the time. He offered me a job there taking my newsletter experience, and doing newsletters for the different plants they had around the country. Well, Data General hit a billion dollars in computer sales during that time. Another one of my jobs was to go online, read all the newspapers every morning: *Wall Street Journal*, [*Worcester*] *Telegram*, *Boston Globe*, take anything related to our business and condense it down into little blips, these little summaries, and then e-mail this out to everybody at the company, the top managers of the company. And at the time that was a really new thing. Computers were so new that the fact that we could do this was huge.

That was a great job, and then from there I just happened to move into some event planning. They would take all of their 10-year employees—because they had so much money at the time—everyone who had been there 10 years, they'd fly them all to Disney World with their families, all expenses paid for a long weekend. So I got involved in coordinating that every year, taking these families to Disney. With this economy, you don't do that today. At the time these companies were booming, and computer technology was booming, so I was there for a few years. Then Thom McAn called me back, and said would you come back as the director of public relations? And it was almost the case where, you almost had to leave to come back. I think if I had stayed in communications there doing the newsletter, I probably would have stayed in communications. But the fact that I left and went into high tech [technology] for a while, I was able to go back at a much higher level. So, I was there as director of public relations and communications and event planning until '91 [1991].

I'm so blessed. Honest to God, because I've always loved what I do, and if you can get paid to do something you love, it doesn't get better than that. That was a great job, and I only left that because I had kids. I stayed home with the kids for 13 years. See that was the tough thing. Here I had this job that I absolutely adored, but I couldn't travel. Had a baby and that was when women were trying to have it all, and it's really hard, and I desperately wanted to keep my job. But I also wanted to stay home so Thom McAn said, "Well let's see if we can make this work, and you can just be a consultant." So for a year I tried working, juggling the two and, to be honest, I just couldn't do it. I couldn't travel, I really wanted to be home, and I felt like I was doing neither job as well as I wanted to. So I left Thom McAn and stayed home for 13 years, which turned out to be great. That was exactly what I needed to do, and it was fabulous, but it was a wonderful job and I hated to leave it.

The personal cost is you sacrifice the income to stay home. That was my choice to do that. And professionally you worry; alright, now I've been out of the workforce for 13 years, right? How am I going to get back in? So, it's not an easy decision to make. It was the best one I made, but it definitely for a woman, it's challenging to figure out how to balance those.

And now the job that I'm in is part time, and when I went back to work that is the perfect way to juggle family and work. I'm the executive director of the Holden Area Chamber of Commerce. So what that means is I'm the only employee in an organization that is basically a volunteer organization. I cover the towns of Holden, Princeton, Paxton, and Rutland. We have 150 businesses, who pay a membership fee to belong. And our challenge is to get those businesses to network amongst themselves. We do a lot of community events. We do Holden Days, which is an enormous community event in town that draws probably 10,000 people from the surrounding area. But basically my job is to promote businesses. I'm the host of a TV show. We visit three of our members every month. So the TV show is great fun, it's one of the best parts of my job. It's a great way to meet people, it helps the community, and it helps the businesses.

Right now I'm active in my church. I serve at the Mustard Seed, which is feeding the hungry. Our church supplies the meal and we take it down there and feed some 300 people who come in off the streets. In the Episcopal Church we have a memorial garden. People who are cremated are buried in this garden. My dad is buried in that garden. I'm one of the trustees of the garden just to keep it up. I've always believed in volunteering, and I've always done it in some form.

Success to me is if you could get paid to do something you love, that's great, you know? And so, if you're enjoying what you're doing and you're healthy. So, I'd say I'm successful. I mean everybody wants to do well and make money, but that's not the be all and end all. You make those choices. I gave up the money in order to stay home with the kids. My choices were the right ones for me, and they're not for everybody! And I'm not saying that women can't work and have kids. They can. I just couldn't. It involved travel and it was just too much.

Audrey Silveri
Age 77
Interviewed on
November 22, 2010 by
Melissa McLain and
Paige Anderson of
Assumption College
Overseen by Prof. Jim
Lang, Assumption
College

I'm a lifelong student. I was at home with my children and then I developed the desire to be a nurse. I went to Mount Wachusett Community College and got an RN [Registered Nurse degree]. Assumption College had the BSN [Bachelor of Science in Nursing degree] and you could come in and use the credits that you had, and work toward a BSN, so I came to Assumption College and I got a BSN in nursing.

It was in 1986. And then I went to Boston College and got a master's in nursing. And then, I got into teaching, and if you teach, you need a doctorate, so I went to the University of Massachusetts in Amherst and I got a doctorate, just in 2002. It was in education. I've always played catch up. My whole life I've been playing catch up.

My husband was a mentor, I guess, to me. I don't know if all husbands are, but when I went back to school and I got my RN degree, I thought that was enough, I wasn't going to do anymore. I was just going to be an RN, and he kept pushing me. Because he taught at Assumption he said, "No you have to go to Assumption, you have to get a BSN." [I said], "I don't want to go." [laughs] He kept nagging me, so I did. He was very supportive all through this up to the point that when I went finally in my old age to go to—a lot of it was in my old age—to get the doctorate over in Amherst, we had to drive over there and the classes were at night and that's a long way. It's a long dark way. I went there for a couple of classes and I said, "I can do the work, but I can't do the commute. It's dark at night and I'm coming home at 11 on the back roads." So he drove me for the rest of the time, which was several years. And he didn't feel like doing that and when he got over there, I had two or three-hour classes, he just had to hang out. So he was a very, very big mentor to me.

Well, my mother was a teacher so I wanted to be a teacher and that was acceptable to my family. But when I was young, I also thought I wanted to be a nurse, but I was just discouraged from doing that. After I had my children, I just became very interested in being a nurse. I have the idea that things that you want to do in your childhood are really deep rooted and eventually you'll do them, even if you don't do them right away. I think that goals that you have in childhood are true goals, and you eventually work your way through to them, even though you might have a lot of detours along the way. I certainly have a lot of detours [laughs].

And then I started teaching at Mount Wachusett Community College. And I liked teaching and I liked nursing, so to combine them was really a very nice thing. So I taught at Mount Wachusett and then I taught at Worcester State College, in the nursing program. And then I became the director of a nursing program at Anna

Maria College, which was a BSN program, and I retired from that last year. And, in fact, I have a job now, [laughs] believe it or not. It's a part-time job, it's at the [University of Massachusetts] Medical School where they have a Graduate School of Nursing, and I have a very-part time job there teaching psychiatric nursing.

I was home with my children until my youngest one was in first grade. And then I went to nursing school. And my youngest child has never forgiven me for that. It's funny, well maybe she has now, but [laughs] for many years she was like, "You stayed at home with all the others and when I went to school …" Well, I figured I had to or else I never would. At that point, I was getting on, you know.

They had chores from the earliest moment that they could, which is about three. A kid of three can do some little chores. They can get stuff for you and they can help you set up the table. They can, and they actually like to, so we, every week we would post a list of chores on the refrigerator, and they changed so it wasn't always the same old chores. I think that's really important for kids.

I always cooked. And I was lucky because my husband, being a professor, was home a lot. He came home earlier than most people would who work 9 to 5. He was very good with the chores, very, very helpful so that was fine and I was staying home. I mean if you're staying home, you can manage. I'm very sensitive on this because my own mother didn't stay home. My mother was a teacher, and she went back to work when I was about 20 months old. But I can remember that. I can remember when she went back to work and how I hated it, screamed and yelled. I always felt close to my aunts, almost closer than my mother, and it wasn't until I was quite old that I realized, of course you are because they took care of you when you were little. That's really strange. I was determined to stay home and I was lucky enough to do it, but those were times when you could.

I let the house go [laughs]. You have to do your job, and you have to be up on that. You can't let that go and you have to eat well, so those things we did. I don't think you should stay up all night cleaning either so we always got enough sleep, but the house suffered.

So I feel very blessed that I was able to stay home. I mean, it was tight, the money was very tight. A professor doesn't make a lot of money and we were pretty poor. We never went hungry, we always ate well, we always had a house in a good neighborhood, but we certainly didn't have a lot of other stuff. We didn't have a lot of clothes. In the fall, we would buy 100 pounds of potatoes, and 50 pounds of onions, and vast quantities of apples, and my husband used to buy these huge wheels of cheese [laughs].

I really think it's a series of challenges and as you go along, you successfully negotiate some of these challenges, and then there are more, there are harder ones, different ones. And so you constantly [are] meeting challenges in life and you have to face up to them and do them. But they keep getting harder, or maybe they don't keep getting harder, but [laughs] you get tired.

Diane Morin
Age 54
Interviewed on April 26, 2006 by
Stephanie Morin of Worcester
State University
Overseen by Prof. Lisa Krissoff
Boehm, Worcester State
University

I grew up in the Greendale section of Worcester, on Sunrise Ave., which is right off of Ararat Street. There were lots of children. My grandparents lived there. My grandfather worked at Norton's [Norton Company] and owned one of the houses up there, lots of young families in the area. So [I] had a lot of children to play with.

I was always busy. We didn't have Internet and very limited TV. At the time TV was black and white, not color. We played jacks, jumped rope, went to ballgames, softball games, baseball games at Kendrick Field. There used to be Norton Field there where they had ball games. Riding bikes all over the place, reading books, playing school. We used to line up all our stuffed animals, and we'd be the teachers. My father used to do a lot of sawing with wood, making things with wood, and there'd be a lot of sawdust around, so my friends and I would play in the sawdust, make sawdust pies, and all these different things with sawdust.

I went to Forest Grove Junior High, and then on to Burncoat Senior High. No college. I started work in high school, maybe my junior year, I think it was. I worked with a friend. Her father owned a printing company, and he used to send out brochures for different areas, and he'd have a mailing list. My job there was to basically type out envelopes and stuff them.

I think I was probably 16, 17, somewhere around there. Before that I got a little work experience by being a candy striper at Hahnemann Hospital. I worked there for maybe about a year—working in the coffee shops, delivering mail, flowers, that sort of thing. And then that company that was the printing shop went out of business. From there I went to another company, also in Worcester, by the name of Hanson Stainless Steel. I worked there doing inventory and secretarial work, and at that point I was also laid off from that place because they were going under, and they closed. So those two places have closed.

While I was still in high school, I started working for Paul Revere [Insurance Company]; they were looking for a typist. And upon graduation, they offered me a full-time job, so instead of going to college, I remained at Paul Revere. And back in those days companies would train you, on-the-job training. From there I was a supervisor of many units on my way up to being middle management. I was billing supervisor, correspondence supervisor, single-issue supervisor, premium collections supervisor. I went on to be a group department specialist, and in that capacity I would work with the law department to make sure that we were following the law.

After I had my first child, I cut back a few hours, still maintained 30 hours, but wanted to be home more with him. And then I got pregnant with my second child, and before I went back to work, found out I was pregnant with a third one, and decided to give my notice. From there, I took three years off and decided to go back to work after those three years—part-time so I could be home with the kids. My husband worked days, so I took a night job. He got home a little bit after the time I had to leave, so I would have a sitter come in from the time that I left until the time that he got home, and I would work 'til about 10:00, 10:30. And that lasted for quite a few years, and I'm still there. My part-time job when I went back was at a supermarket, at Big Y. Started out as a cashier; went on to learn the booth, the safe, payroll, and administrative work there, and that's where I still am on a part-time basis.

Back in my day, it was a little bit easier; things didn't, I don't think, cost quite as much. The idea was to stay at home with the kids. Where today things cost so much—you buy a house, a family has to have two jobs, and if they do have kids, that's even more of an expense, so it might be two jobs plus another job. I would wish that we didn't have to. Material things [are] unimportant to me. I'd rather stay home and not work, and make sure the kids are watched out for, and I'll make sacrifices and do away with some of the things I'd like to do rather than have to go to work while the kids are growing up. It's something that you have to do; it's a necessity. In today's world it's more or less both parents chipping in doing housework, raising the kids. It's not like in the '50s where the mom's home all the time and can do all this stuff. Where *both* parents are putting in a 40-hour week, it really has to be a shared thing.

Michelle Jones-Johnson
Interviewed on November 3, 2013 by Lauren Moreira and Ricky Gonzalez of Assumption College
Overseen by Profs. Leslie Choquette and Allison Meyer, Assumption College

I attended University of Michigan right around the time when affirmative action was [in full swing and it provided increased opportunities for students of color to attend the university]. There was a constant challenge of attempting to overcome the perception that the only reason why I was there, was because I was a [student of color]. When I was growing up, my father and I would take drives to Ann Arbor on the weekends. I would always say to my dad, "I'm going to be a student here," and he would say, "Yes, you will." He encouraged me [to visualize that] at a very young age. I applied to only one college, unlike everyone else.

So the challenge was how to attend an institution that [prestigious] and large while dealing with the dynamics [of race and culture]. I remember sitting in a lecture room with maybe 400 students and being the only African-American student in the room and intensely feeling the pressure to perform exceptionally well. I definitely felt more pressure because if I didn't go to class, they knew I wasn't there [laughs]. So I couldn't skip classes or check out early.

My family experienced financial difficulties after my freshman year. I went to speak with someone in the Financial Aid [Department]. I will never forget what one of the counselors said to me, "Well, we don't have any other options for you." They asked, "What? You can't play a sport or something [to get an athletic scholarship]?" and I said, "No, I don't play sports." The assumption that I should be able to play a sport because I was Black [took me by surprise], and I just thought it spoke volumes about the challenges many of us faced. The individual I spoke to was another person of color and that's what really hurt. I ended up leaving there for a year, and I remember thinking, "I'm sorry I don't play competitive sports." [I was too focused on my studies] and not coordinated enough to do both [laughs]. [I returned a year later and graduated on time.]

Oh absolutely, absolutely [it's a challenge to be a person of color and a woman in the workplace]. As you progress in your career, you start to recognize different things. Because you've gone through different challenges you are much more equipped to deal with certain situations. I remember the year I had to leave college, I worked at an accounting firm. I was a secretary, and I remember going in and thinking I'm pretty smart, I can do some stuff, right? But I was making coffee, typing, and running errands. The guys would come in and think I was just capable of making the coffee, and because it was my first professional job, I thought [eventually I'd be valued for my skills and education]. I remember a few years later, after graduating from college, working for a law firm and that's where I started my HR [human resources] role. One of the partners had an issue with one of his staff and called down to HR and said, "I need you to run up here." I go up there and he's going on and on about his assistant, "I want her fired today and I want her out of here!" I told him that I would have a conversation with his staff person. Then he [demands] that I get him some coffee. So I told him that I would be happy to get someone on his staff to get his coffee. So it's learning how to handle those situations as tactfully and professionally as possible, understanding the politics and dynamics around it and not take it personally. I don't take on other people's issues, so I let them work that out. I'm focused on doing my job. But it's a challenge [to be a woman of color in the workplace], it continues to be a challenge, it's always something that will be with me. I am always going to be a woman, and I am always going to be a person of color. You can't change those dynamics, so you learn to deal with it [and embrace who you are].

My husband is the president of a college [Becker College]. I had a career when we arrived, and planned to continue to work. I sense that it's very hard for some to understand my drive to move forward with my career. I think that is where some of the stereotypes come in, in terms of being female and having your husband being in a very prominent role. Some assume that my job is to take care of the home and be there to support him. I agree with the supporting part, but I've worked since I was probably a junior in high school, and having that level of independence is important to me. It is also important for me to work, so my kids can see that you have to work every day, really hard. So now that they are college students, [they understand the sacrifice needed to get what you want in life.]

I serve on a lot of different boards including the Hanover Theatre and the Reliant Foundation Board. I try to do as much as I can, but my challenge is that I have a lot on my plate, and I work full time, I have two kids. I consider myself an ambassador for Becker College, and that comes with a lot of responsibility [and commitment]. I try to [support many initiatives] in the community. I guess I should also cook dinner once in a while [laughs]. It becomes a lot and I wonder how I get it all done. We've always been involved in the community, that's never been a question. I think now that I have a better sense of my role in my profession, and at the college, I have to think about what makes more sense in terms of my community work.

I am trying to think back to conversations with the kids to see if they ever expressed feeling traumatized by something [laughs]. I think we did a good job carving time out for what is important, especially since I was in graduate school when they were young. I think our daughter was probably five or six when I completed my first master's degree, and then in middle and high school when I was working on my MBA. I do not think either of our kids felt like I was neglecting them, but trying to better things for our family. At a certain age all they really wanted me for was a ride to the game and a cell phone [laughs]. They had their own social lives, and they were old enough to be supportive. If I was studying and the phone was ringing, they would say, "Sorry, she's studying." I believe they are proud of me. [My drive to continue my education and career did not necessarily cause a problem in terms of family priorities.] I just think they understood that this was something that was important for me to do, as an individual, as a woman, in support of my family. It would be interesting to see what they would say [laughs] now as adults. I think the cooking, or lack thereof, was the issue more than anything else.

There are going to be challenges in everything that you do. No matter who you are, what you are, how much you make, how much money you don't have, you are always going to have your challenges. I think your lens is different if you're a woman or a person of color. I think you look at things in life in a different light [based on your own individual journey], but the challenges still remain. That is the part I was telling you about, enjoy this time now, because there are peaks and valleys in life, it's a continuum.

Gloria Abramoff
Age 55
Interviewed on October 22, 2007 by Kayla Haveles of
College of the Holy Cross
Overseen by Prof. Stephanie Yuhl, College of the Holy
Cross

It was a wonderful bookstore. It started very small. I'll give the whole history of the bookstore. When [my husband] opened it in 1975, it was 600 square feet, just tiny. And he and his partner were the entire staff. And then I came in. He bought out his partner, and we eventually had one or two employees. We bought the building next to us, and then we expanded into the basement, and then we expanded into the upstairs and I— I always laugh—I had a customer who told me once he had a nightmare that we were tunneling under Chandler Street because we maxed out this sort of funny storefront at Tatnuck Square. And about 16 years ago, we bought an old factory building on Chandler Street, about two miles away from Tatnuck Square. Although we kept the name, Tatnuck Bookseller, we were no longer in Tatnuck Square, but it was [the] Sleeper and Hartley building. It's about 22,000 square feet, and it was at the time the largest independent bookseller in New England, before the big box [stores] came in. Although we still physically, I think, were larger than some of the ones in the Worcester area. Oh, we had a full service restaurant. They served three meals a day, and you could get a martini, and we ran, at one point, the WPI [Worcester Polytechnic Institute] bookstore, the Clark [University] bookstore, and the Becker [College] bookstore. And now, we don't! [Laughs] It's a changing marketplace. But yeah, it was a great adventure; it was a great adventure. And it was a wonderful store.

I hadn't planned on some hugely hard-driving career, if you want to know the truth. I'm really not that aggressive. So, bookselling for me was a wonderful career. And getting to be the boss, and not within a huge corporate structure, it was heaven. It was pretty great. Because if you are the boss at Barnes and Noble, I mean, you are within these really strict parameters. They tell you the how, and the why, and the what, and the when of everything you do, and we were always winging it. I was not a born salesman, but I'll tell you, this was a product I could get behind [laughs]. It was pretty great.

That's not to say there weren't times of great stress, because having kids does that to you anyway, and having a business does that to you, and having a husband does that to you [laughs]. But there was never any question that if I needed to be home with the kids, I'd stay home, because his interests and my interests definitely coincided there. And having grandparents around also was really nice then, because [they would be there] if there were any kind of emergency, that's also the upside to living in your hometown. Here I have other people who know your children's best interest, and who are incredibly close to their hearts. I certainly saw lots of women really struggling with that. It was hard. It's hard for them, and it was hard for us. Because we were so close to our business, and knew it was easier for us in terms of childrearing, we tried to be really nice to people about that. But in retail, you can't put the job aside until the next day. If you're supposed to be there opening the store or running the register—it's not like a paper-pushing job. You can't pile it up on your desk and say, "Well today isn't a good day for it, but tomorrow is." You physically really have to be there. And there was not much telecommuting then, but you really couldn't have done it.

When the kids were very young, particularly the first one because this was before I had two, I took him to work. And he had his little playpen in the bookstore. The store was small, I was young, he was cute [laughs]. It was good for business. But once they got older, they both had family daycare. Not my family, but they were both in daycare situations for most of their babyhoods until they went to school. So I could beat myself up all day about whether it was wonderful or not so wonderful. I mean they were nice ladies who took care of them. I have no horror stories [laughs].

Susan Scully-Hill
Age 45
Interviewed on March 25, 2009
by Melissa Anello and Courtney
Foley of Assumption College
Overseen by Profs. Linda
Ammons and Leslie Choquette,
Assumption College

I was born in South Amboy [New Jersey] and when my parents got divorced, my mom moved to Michigan with all of us kids. The automotive industry was in Michigan and the Detroit area, and she felt that she would be able to get a job, and she could support us on her own. Another thing that also concerned my mom was that we would be able to go to college, and in Michigan there were a lot of state schools. So she thought that we would better be able to afford to go to college, and we would have more college options than living in New Jersey. I got all my degrees from Michigan State. So when I was graduating with my PhD in 1996, I started looking for jobs.

Having a bachelor's degree in social work and looking at the prospect of not being able to support myself with what I could make, definitely presented a kind of challenge. I did work after I graduated with my bachelor's degree as a nanny. Then I did work after my master's degree for two years as a professional counselor, but professionally I guess when I really started working, was probably in 1996. In '96 I graduated with my PhD, and I worked as a professor at Emporia State University.

It doesn't feel like work to me. I mean it's hard work and it's demanding, but it's a career. It's very much part of my identity. And I feel like probably one of the most blessed people in the whole world. I mean, I want to win the lottery, but [laughs] barring that. No, really that could not have ever done for me what being in this career has done for me. And I guess really the most poignant thing that I can say about it is that it's so much intertwined with who I am that it's not necessarily my job, like, "Oh, I've got to go to work today." It is just so integrated with who I am, but also with my family and so many areas of my life. I'm so rewarded by my relationship with students, seeing how they grow, and how they develop, and what they learn. But they also have influenced my life, too, tremendously for how I've grown and what I have learned. So, not many people get to always be meeting and forming relationships. Ninety-nine percent of the students are phenomenal human beings. They are so interesting and so stimulating to know. Who gets to do that? And get paid and sort of have wonderful work arrangements, too, because I have a lot of flexibility. I still can be the primary caretaker for my kids, be a full-time mom for them, and get to do something I love and that continues to challenge me intellectually. Because if I want to learn something new, or teach a new course, or try something different, then I can do it. I don't have to do it only this way. So, aside from being able to be with my kids and my family, it's great.

I don't know that I have always [balanced responsibilities and priorities in my life]. That's the really, really, really hard part, and I think that as women, it's so much harder for us. And I'm not going to beat on men or be negative at all about a man's role in life, but it's very challenging to find balance, if not impossible to find balance and I, as a woman, continually feel that I'm not doing enough, or I'm not good enough, or I feel guilt if I shortchange one area in my life, or one person in my life. And sometimes it does get upsetting and frustrating when it feels like as a woman, you feel like you have to do so much more to be viewed as equal or as competent as a male counterpart. And we balance so many things. Even though I have a rather egalitarian relationship with my husband, the bottom line is I'm the mom. When the kids are sick at school, I have to pick them up, and I am home with them. I help them with their homework. I know everything that is going on in their lives. You try to share more things or responsibilities, but predominantly the burden falls to the woman or the mom. Sometimes too, there's even that well I can't do something, I can't stay, I'm sorry I have to get out of here at this time because my kids are coming home and I need to help them with their homework, I need to get them to activities. There isn't tremendous understanding or I haven't experienced tremendous understanding from colleagues or people who say that that's valued. "What do you mean you have to leave at three?" or "What do you mean you're leaving now?" And that happens to me a lot. That's sort of a personal trigger button, "Oh, you're leaving now?" "Well, it's 3:00 and then I go to my other job which goes until the kids go to bed." And so sometimes I just think that we have a heavy burden.

I think in some way that although things have changed and we really have moved forward in so many ways with regard to women's rights, equality, and opportunity for women, that there are still challenges, many challenges that lie ahead. We talked about finding balance, being viewed as competent. There is still a lot of bias, gender inequity, and gender bias. I mean, there is still a lot.

Life will be challenging and the whole trying to achieve balance and feeling that you're a good mom, you're a good sister, you're a good daughter, you're a good wife, those things can kind of make us crazy when we're all trying to be so good in all of those roles, and there is so much work that goes along with that. Don't despair and don't let that get you down. The experience of being all of those things is so rewarding and so significant, and mostly I think what comes to mind is the experience of being a mom. And although I will fail at times—I'm thinking about five loads of laundry and homework and everything—the role that a woman plays in her family is irreplaceable. Because I don't want to say a man can't do it, I'm not saying that, but it's just that that is so rewarding. The relationships, the connections, how your children feel about you, how your family members feel about you are all the things that are worthwhile.

Judith Savageau
Age 56
Interviewed on April 10,
2012 by Lane Bennett and
Kyle Gallivan of
Assumption College
Overseen by Prof. Carl
Keyes, Assumption
College

So I'm an epidemiologist and biostatistician— sometimes I use these titles because they relate to the research I do. I also teach a lot here at the [University of Massachusetts] Medical School, so sometimes I use my faculty title. I'm an associate professor of Family Medicine and Community Health. I really wanted to be public health and population based, not individual person based, and that's what made me decide to go to public health school as opposed to going to medical school. Besides being here in Family Medicine, I'm down the street in Shrewsbury at the Center for Health Policy and Research.

I now get to do health policy research which really has a lot of impact from a public health standpoint. So, I think I'm really lucky. I think I have lots of choices, and I'm never going to complain about that [laughs].

There are certainly a lot of opportunities in an academic environment for Worcester [women], and certainly UMass has also really been pushing for more diversity, not only in terms of women faculty, but diversity from racial and ethnic groups. So I think there are opportunities for women. Do we have to seek them out a little more? I think the reality is, and I don't mind mentioning this on tape, you know if you're a woman with children, you are the primary caregiver to them. So there are decisions I have had to make in my own life. Absolutely people who are my colleagues, [who] are basically the same age as I am, probably are at least a step or a half step or a little bit ahead of me. But I made a decision [about] having my kids, being available to my kids, and about working here in Family Medicine. I never could sit at a place and look back and say, "Gosh, I wish I had written one more paper for a medical journal." As many papers as I've written, I never wanted to say that, but I would have hated if I [said], "I wish I had gone to that field hockey game." I never had a choice knowing that people will probably leap a little bit ahead of me, but I think that's just how you balance family and work. I don't think a lot of men have to do [that].

I was a work-study student [at the National Braille Press] for four years in college. And I ended up working there for a year [after graduation]. It actually merged with what is now the Massachusetts Association for the Blind. I now sit on the board of the Massachusetts Association for the Blind, and so it's kind of come full circle from a job that I had 30 years ago.

I'm not somebody who believes in fate. We mostly have control over our lives, but if there's any sort of fate to life, having spent all that time working at

National Braille Press, and Mass. Association for the Blind, [and] I became a braille transcriber for the Library of Congress—my first-born child is visually impaired. He was born with a very, very rare eye disorder, and now has very limited vision. I think it's really kind of odd that [laughs] sort of investing all your time, and that's certainly what kept me very involved in the vision community, and the blindness community, is more because of him than anything else. It's something I could bring a history of knowledge and skills to. All of a sudden my personal [life] had this issue that [I] never expected would happen.

It's a huge amount of work to have a child with any kind of a disability. I was a founder, with two other parents, of a nonprofit called the Massachusetts Association for Parents of the Visually Impaired, to really be a resource for other parents. I needed to learn from parents whose kids were a few years ahead of my kids. It really gave me an opportunity—from an advocacy standpoint—to just make a big impact.

Most important to me is community service. The woman who founded, I believe it's Save the Children, Marian Wright Edelman, has this great quote that "Service is the rent we pay for living here on this planet." And I am an avid believer. I do five to 10 hours a week of community service. A lot of it is related to vision. A lot are projects at my church related to Hope for Housing Project that the Massachusetts Housing Alliance does. I do a lot of work with food pantries here in Worcester, because I think hunger is very much related to health. I think that if you can't find an hour a week to volunteer, then you're really not looking. When my kids were little, I volunteered at their school, I helped with projects, I did things I obviously could at night, I was happy to write a school newsletter, or help coordinate a book sale at school. If you look, there are a million things you can do out there. And I got my kids engaged probably from the minute they hit elementary school. And they both do lots of community service as well. I live to serve. It sounds really hokey, but I think why we're here is to help somebody else.

My kids didn't really get to know their grandparents very well, so that was another attraction to moving back here. But then they started having their own health issues, you know, just as you're getting older. So did that really personally affect my life? Probably not as much, until it got to the point where there were enough health issues that you were part of what people now call now that "sandwich generation." Here I am raising children and then taking care of parents on the other end of things. I think that's where it has had some impact on how your life progresses, and what you can get done in any given day, and thinking about their mortality. And that at some point your parents aren't going to be here and that's what happened, and my kids don't have any grandparents now.

I still think, though, that if you want to balance work and life, there are decisions you have to make as a woman. I think you have to have that conscious decision as you're making choices about what you're going to do, how much do you want to balance, how much do you want to have a life outside of work, and how do you want to balance that? I think women have to make many more decisions than men do in terms of timing of having children, and when that's going to work well, if you have a trajectory in place for yourself. The fact that we actually consciously think about that is really kind of odd [laughs], that women do that. I don't think men ever think about that to the same degree that women do. There are opportunities there that maybe never were there decades ago, but if you really want to have a nice work/life balance, then you do have to consciously make decisions about that depending on where you see yourself. And those kinds of weird questions: Where do you think you're going to be in 10 years, or 20 years? Where do you want to be? There's a lot of stuff you have to give up in order to get something else and so, I just think family first. I think we need to work to live, not live to work and so that's just a conscious decision that I think women have to make.

I remember years ago when my second child was born, we were living in Rochester, New York. I had always gotten favorable and outstanding reviews, and I got sort of an average review one year and I was just really shocked. And I worked for a woman; she was my immediate supervisor and she'd had kids of her own, and she specifically said to me it was because I had been on maternity leave. And I thought, "Well what do you mean?" And she said, "Well you weren't as productive as your colleagues." And I said, "I was on maternity leave—I mean I can't believe I'm being dinged for this." And she said, "Well, when you think about the stuff that you've accomplished in volume, it was less than x, y and z person"—you know, in the offices next to me. And I said, "But I did everything that was asked to be done—I excelled at everything that I did." And she said, "I made a choice not to give you certain projects because I knew that you would be out for maternity leave, and so I had to reset deadlines." I said, "That was a choice you made."

Here I was being punished for taking that time off, and so in some ways, I don't think that's really changed in some regard, but do we have to own that ourselves? I think that is a societal issue. I think women should feel powerful that they get to give birth [laughs]. You know, men can't do that. [Women] have the ability to do something that is far more important than any job here on this earth. But to this day, do we still not have the same opportunities because we have to make choices in our lives that men don't have to make?

CHAPTER TWO

PASSION PROJECT

It is the ultimate luxury to combine passion and contribution. It's also a very clear path to happiness.

Sheryl Sandberg, CEO of Facebook, activist, author

Annette Rafferty
Age 82
Interviewed on November
15, 2012 by Felicia Tiberi
and Katie Coderre of
Assumption College
Overseen by Profs. Leslie
Choquette and Esteban
Loustaunau, Assumption
College

  I graduated from college in Chicopee, [MA], Our Lady of the Elms. I entered the Sisters of St. Joseph and I went to Holyoke for my boot camp training, as I call it, and then I started 34 years of teaching. After starting

Abby's House, which has become my life's work, I found that I had to make a choice of whether to continue as a nun, or to leave and give full time to this work, which I ended up doing at age 56. It was a huge decision. I love teaching, but I had to make a choice. This work was so all encompassing. So my lifestyle hasn't changed at all, I'm still doing all of those things, but I have the freedom to come and go, and to spend more time in concentrating on developing programs.

If you had known me 50 years ago, I am a different person. I went along with everything. I had so many experiences in my life as a woman, finally I realized that women were truly second-class citizens in every area, and I just began to do more and more in the Women's Movement and was very affected by that and became really an advocate and an activist for women. I literally found my voice. And one of the happiest moments was [when] I was asked to speak at Mechanic's Hall. I shared the stage with Anita Hill. Anita Hill was the woman who held up the confirmation of Clarence Thomas to the Supreme Court, based on her experience of having been sexually harassed by him in the workplace. She's become a poster woman, so to speak, for advances in [the handling of] sexual harassment [cases] for women. She spoke on the stage, and I spoke with her. It was a defining moment for me because she had found her voice, and she didn't want to concentrate on the bad treatment that she [had received.] Watch those hearings to see how badly she was treated by the senators. I had written my first book, *Wearing Smooth the Path* for women, and I told the story of my experience starting Abby's, and we connected. I mean I did a little tiny thing, and she did a great big thing. But the point was we were both advocates for women in a different range of influence and in different spheres. I did become a girl who [was] quiet and afraid to raise her hand, to [a woman] who was an activist for women.

I think the biggest influence on me was the treatment I felt I experienced trying to get Abby's started for women, and also Marilyn French's book *The Women's Room*. I remember reading it and immediately joining the National Organization for Women, and I've had a membership there for over 40 years because I think they stand up for women in the face of all kinds of oppression. My appearing with [Anita Hill] was a confirmation that yes indeed, something had happened to me. That there had been that "aha" moment when you know that something has happened to you, and that you could never go back to where you were before.

I have two master's degrees from Assumption [College] and I did graduate work at B.C. [Boston College] and St. John's University in New York, and Notre Dame [University] in Indiana and I did a lot of workshops. I was very much influenced by feminist theology. I went out to study community organizing, and I took a side course with feminist theology, and both of them influenced my life. They were probably the two biggest academic influences in my life. The biggest influence was just my own personal experiences.

[I founded Abby's House] with a group of women. I was kind of a catalyst. I was invited to be on a committee in the city that was investigating the claims that there were women and children in the street. A couple of pastors were getting phone calls [asking them if they] could pick up somebody that was thrown out of the house, or was just wandering around the city. So I was asked to serve on this group, Urban Ministry Commission, and I took the work very seriously. I had a full-time job, but I needed to explore this because I had always wanted the sisters—and I was still a sister of St. Joseph at that time—I wanted the sisters to become more involved with other women. I thought other women had so much to teach us about life, and about themselves, and about ourselves, that we needed to know, and so I jumped at the opportunity to do that. And I took the work seriously. I went to neighborhood centers, to family help centers, to women that I knew were social workers, and we finally gathered together enough documentation that there was indeed a need for women to have a temporary emergency shelter. The group decided not to proceed at that time with the shelter. But this is where I couldn't turn back. I knew they were out there.

Nineteen seventy-three was the year I started to do all this work. They needed someone to spearhead it, so I did. In the fall of '75 we met and there were about 68 women who showed up and about four men. We divided up the work that we knew needed to be done. We had a financial committee raising money, a committee to do publicity, a committee to look into spaces that we might be able to rent, and we just went at it. By the end of April 1976 we had enough money for maybe a couple months' rent; we had enough people willing to give a couple nights a month to staff the shelter. We found a place, and the landlord let us have two floors of this beautiful old home in a Crown Hill neighborhood. This is now a historic neighborhood. He gave us the two floors for 325 [dollars] a month including heat and light. And I guess that was the beginning of it. We kept fundraising, we kept at it, and we opened the doors on June 7, 1976, and the shelter doors have never closed since. And in addition to the one building, we now have three others for permanent housing. So we have four buildings under the umbrella of one house. So it was the work of the community; it was the work of a lot of individuals, a lot of civic groups, a lot of church groups, a lot of schools. I just happened to be the one that pushed it to get it done and it got done and they made me the founder, but I think the whole community were actually founders; they all founded. That's how we got started—40 years next year, I mean for me, and it will be 37 for Abby's.

Abby Kelley Foster was Worcester's most famous abolitionist and women's rights activist. But she'd fallen into anonymity and her history was kind of lost, like a lot of women's histories. So our shelter for women was named Abby Kelley Foster, and that's how we are recorded at the State House for our papers. We shortened it to Abby's House because when we opened, people began to call to place kids there. They thought it was a foster home, because no one recognized her name.

I wrote the two books because I didn't want anyone to forget what went into founding Abby's House and to recognize as many of the volunteers by name and the groups by name. The first one was *Wearing Smooth the Path: The First 25 Years at Abby's* and the second title is *Still Wearing Smooth the Path: The Last Ten Years.* The wording of the book, *Wearing Smooth the Path,* comes from a speech that Abby gave at the second National Woman's Conference at Brinley Hall in Worcester in which she got up to give a speech. She was a fiery woman, and she stood up and she said something like this, "Bloody feet, sisters, have worn smooth the path by which you have come hither." In other words, it's been no easy journey to get from where I started to where I am now, and when Margaret LaRue, the proofreader and editor of the first book saw the phrase "have worn smooth the path" she said, "Well isn't Abby's House wearing smooth the path for women and children?" And hence was born the title, and it came right out of that second National Woman's Conference here [in Worcester]. So we're still wearing smooth the path and it's—and bloody feet, yes I said that, and bloody feet—it's been a hard journey to get from there to where we are now, but it's been even harder for the women who come through. But we have made it smoother for them to get from A to B and then from B to C. It's not a dead-end place; we encourage them to get educated, to find jobs, to get out, to put their names into

Worcester housing, so that eventually they can have their own place.

I am a great prayer. I pray all the time, not maybe formal prayers, I talk to myself, I pray, I have a great devotion to Mary and I pray every night to her and I look at the lives of the women around me at Abby's House, women who for the grace of God are alive. I don't know how I could survive the way some of them survived. So I get through the tough times through pushing ahead, wearing smooth the path for myself, asking Mary who in my mind was just a very ordinary Jewish woman who did an extraordinary thing in probably very difficult times. I have that devotion to her. But I think mostly I get my inspiration along with that from the women I work with at Abby's and the staff, and the volunteers. I'm more of a half-full person—glass half-full than half-empty—so that comes from being with those women.

Joan Webster
Age 74
Interviewed on November 13,
2006 by Lindsay Schoen and
Leslie Lupien of Assumption
College
Overseen by Prof. Brian Niece,
Assumption College

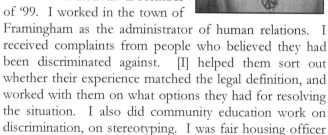

    I retired in December of '99. I worked in the town of Framingham as the administrator of human relations. I received complaints from people who believed they had been discriminated against. [I] helped them sort out whether their experience matched the legal definition, and worked with them on what options they had for resolving the situation. I also did community education work on discrimination, on stereotyping. I was fair housing officer for the town. In addition, I was 504 coordinator for the town and that was federal legislation which had to do with disabilities.

The issues of justice, and discrimination, and stereotyping, and inclusion are really kind of a passion [for me]. [When I retired], I was searching all over Worcester to find a group that I could work with. I was getting increasingly frustrated. I was visiting [a friend] on the Cape [who] took me to a U.U. [Unitarian Universalist] church. I was amazed because there was a sense of community. People seemed to care about the same things I cared about. I [now go to the Unitarian Universalist Church] on Holden Street. It seems to fit me, and the sense of community that is there is important to me, and I never thought that I'd find it again.

I went to public schools in Elizabeth, New Jersey. When the high school became too small, [and the city] needed to build a new high school, it seemed to them that if they segregated by gender, that it would be cheaper. Everyone knew we weren't going to use the automotive shop, and boys wouldn't use sewing and cooking, and you wouldn't have to have two sets of restrooms. So they built a new school, and the new school was built for the boys, and the old school was given to the girls. And it led to kind of interesting experiences for the girls because the boys couldn't take all the leadership positions; there weren't any [boys]. And so things that in co-ed schools frequently girls don't have a shot at, at an all-girls school we all did everything. We didn't quite know what to do with our leadership skills because there were our mothers telling us we had to hide that kind of thing. Can't let them know that. Can't let them know that you're smarter than they are either. And that was the mood when I was growing up. You hid certain things, like your ability, definitely, definitely, your ability and your smarts.

When I got to college, I was bedazzled by the opportunities that there were. One of the questions I asked was if there was a literary magazine because I was interested in writing. And there were a couple of professors who said, "No, but there should be. Why don't you do a survey?" Now I was a freshman and I didn't know what was going on, but they said, "Why don't you do a survey and we'll help." So coming from that, I accidentally started the literary magazine on the Clark campus [laughs]. Being curious about the world really does lead to getting involved. I got involved in the newspaper too, of course.

Actually my being involved in politics goes back before college. I remember going to New York City for meetings of something called The World Federalists, which was a one-world government group. When I was 16, I terrified my parents because it was 1948, and in the election of '48 there was a third party called the Progressive Party, and I became a Young Progressive.

I guess the most coherent activity that I was involved with was an attempt to do voter registration in Fayette County, Tennessee. And in the '60s, I was the mother of young children—had all kinds of things going on, so I was not a good candidate to going down myself. But what we did was a whole variety of ways of supporting that project. We would host some of the folks who were the people who lived there, and needed time out. And we'd bring them up to Cortland, which is right near Ithaca where Cornell is, and there was a kind of a support group out in Cortland. And we would give them a chance to catch their breath, and also organize events that would be a combination of fundraising, and a chance for people to tell others what was going on, what life was like for them. Some of my friends, some of the people who were teaching at Cortland at the time, actually did go down and came back with bullet holes in their cars. People played rough. And they weren't playing. Then there was an overlap time when the civil rights activities were continuing and anti-war activities were starting, and it got all blended together and a lot of who was active were the same people. The Women's Movement started [and] I knew that I was going to be part of that too.

And so there were several projects that I got involved with, in addition to teaching. As part of the Massachusetts State Advisory Committee to the U.S. Civil Rights Commission, I was one of the people who worked on the booklet for sexual harassment that was aimed at employers to let them know why they needed a policy and what sexual harassment was. I was involved in the American Civil Liberties Union in Vermont, the state affiliate, and I ended up being head of the state affiliate so that I could help get things done. And we ended up doing the first conference that there was in the state on women's issues. And when I was teaching, there were two of us that were interested in teaching a class called "Issues of and About Women." Well, it's hard not to be involved with women's issues. At least, I don't see how you cannot be. By being female you're involved in women's issues, in one way or another. Whether it's formal or not.

I'm not sure about success in my life as a global thing. I know the way I knew a class was successful, when I was teaching, was when it continued after the class ended. A course was successful when it made a difference in what students did when the course was no longer going. As far as a total life goes, I'm not sure how to judge success on that. Maybe it's the human heart, or the willingness to be engaged in the world and in your life, to play and be an active participant in your life rather than passive. And trying to live in a way that's ethical, that's right, that makes some positive contribution, so that you're stomping around on the earth isn't creating damage, but is leaving some decent footprint behind. But I guess I feel as one person, what I can do by myself is very tiny. And that's OK. I guess that's why I look for groups because they can do so much more.

I wanted to talk to [my children] about when I died. My mother died. There was such chaos and I swore that I didn't want my kids subjected to nonsense like what I saw happening. And so, I wanted them to be protected by having talked about everything and capturing things on paper, so that we could talk about what kind of ceremony would be useful to them. Because I figured I'd be dead and gone, and what mattered was what would help them. One of the other things that I wanted to talk about was an anatomical gift. I had seen some of my students, when their parents died, just completely freak out when they discovered that their parents wanted to donate parts of their bodies. And so I wanted to find out what my children's reaction would be. I said, "What would you think of a donation of anything that would be useful, any body parts whatsoever? Would that be OK or not OK?" And one of my sons looked at me and said, "Mom, you've spent your whole life trying to help other people, why would you stop just because you were dead?" [Laughs]

Lynne McKenney Lydick
Age 52
Interviewed on October 9, 2007
by Megan Murphy of College of
the Holy Cross
Overseen by Prof. Stephanie
Yuhl, College of the Holy Cross

I was absolutely not a feminist in college, absolutely not. Nor really an activist at all. I remember one resident assistant who had this bumper sticker on a door "Question Authority." I did not know what that meant. What does that mean, question authority? I had had no clue what that was all about. I had friends who were more active and I think that became a catalyst. Who are your friends and what are they doing? Are they marching in Washington? Who are the important people in your life and what are they doing? My parents were very socially active in organizations that raised funds for very good causes. But activism for women's rights? No. Even though my mother was very independent, in 1973 she still had to get my father to sign the papers if she was going to have a checking account in her name. [You] couldn't open a credit card unless you had your husband's signature. Both my parents were civically involved, so those are role models. My mom didn't work outside the home, but she did a lot of volunteer work. So that always was there, but as far as actually getting out and being vocal and going to Boston and speaking to legislators and making phone calls and calling for candidates and things like that, that didn't come around until we lived here in Worcester, and had friends who were actively involved in politics and human rights issues.

I don't have a paying job outside the home. Although I really shouldn't say that. I'm an actor, so I do several one-woman shows, and a two-person show, and my husband and I do a Christmas show. I have been involved with the Worcester Women's History Project since 1999. I joined their marketing committee in order to promote the Women 2000 Conference that we held here in Worcester [to celebrate] the 150th anniversary of the First National Woman's Rights Convention that was held in Worcester in 1850. So I started with the project in 1999. I have been a member of the Worcester chapter of [the] National Organization for Women and was just elected as an at-large member to the League of Women Voters. My husband and I are both members of the ACLU [American Civil Liberties Union]. I got involved in volunteering for the Red Cross right after [Hurricane] Katrina, and I was working on that quite a bit at the beginning.

But I think the organization that really has my

heart and soul is the Jane Fund. I sit on the board with my husband and nine other board members, and we raise funds for women who can't pay for abortion services. And I think this is going on our fifth year on the board. And we are really looking at what role women play in the world based on how they are regarded, as far as their ovaries are concerned and their uterus, because women are really not in control of their own bodies in this country. In fact, Tom and I went to a conference in Minneapolis because the Jane Fund is a part of the National Network of Abortion Funds. There are 104 funds in 42 different states that do what we do, raise funds for women who cannot afford abortion services. And we went to that conference and you just realize that—and even though we knew this—it was stunning to us that Roe v. Wade was passed in 1973, and three years later the Hyde Amendment came in saying no government money will be used for abortion services. And so the Hyde Amendment is now 31 years old. And women, poor women, are not treated the same way as women who have money in this country. That's not news, but what it comes down to is the basic right to control your body and who has the deciding factor. Should it be those White men in Washington D.C., that are making the laws? So Tom and I are very committed to that particular organization and consider that probably our—that and ACLU, are the top social [justice] organizations that we consider our duty as human beings to participate in.

After Katrina, I hit a point where I just said, "I just have to do everything I can do to help out whoever needs to be helped." So when the kids were at school and when I wasn't in their school doing something, I was filling every single minute with something else that I felt had to be done. I had to be part of the solution to whatever was going on. So I was very involved in a lot of different campaigns, and voter calling, and stuffing envelopes, and dropping literature, and collecting signatures. I think now I have come to a determination that I really need to step back a bit, and focus my energies a little bit more, instead of just doing everything. Do the pieces that I can do. I was going to print this bumper sticker that said, "An activist cannot keep a clean house." I thought that would absolve me and make me feel better. And it did for a while.

One woman who I portray, Abby Kelley Foster, the 19th century abolitionist and women's rights activist, is certainly an inspiration. How she tirelessly did what she did on the road, lecturing at a time when women were supposed to be submissive, and not have minds of their own, and certainly not speaking to mixed audiences [of males and females]. She just did it, she just did it. She was committed to human rights. She was born on the same day as Martin Luther King, Jr. She was born 118 years earlier. And they had the exact same message, human rights. Equality and justice for all. I would have to say she's one of my biggest heroes. And then you say to yourself, "I'm complaining about laundry, the house being a mess, and other people don't have a house." Those are the day-to-day inspirations, the people that keep on. And I know several feminist activists who have spent years [working] for reproductive rights and are still working 30, 40—well they were working before Roe v Wade so 40, 50 years involved with reproductive freedom, and they keep on going. They're inspirational.

Success is really the number of people you touch in your life and making people's lives better—working with people who are dedicated to improving people's lives. I think that's the whole reason we are here, is to leave a legacy of inspiration. I was really honored when a friend of mine was asked why she is active, and she said [it was] because she knew me, and I was [a] role model. To me that is success, because now I have touched her; who in turn will she touch?

Mary Anne Azanza
Age 49
Interviewed on March 30, 2009
by Colleen Quinn and Kara
Shallow of Assumption College
Overseen by Profs. Leslie
Choquette and Linda Ammons,
Assumption College

I finished all my schooling in the Philippines and two years after I graduated from college, I entered religious life. I became a Religious of the Assumption which is an international Catholic congregation. We are in 34 different countries, and one of the countries we're in is the United States. And I was asked in 1996 to join the community here in Worcester as a missionary, with the purpose of beginning some apostolic work with the immigrant community in Worcester, and with the poor and with the local church. Even if our sisters had always been at Assumption College from the time they came to Worcester, they wanted one of us to work outside of the college and to engage Assumption College students in the inner city of Worcester. So I came in '96 and I started working at St. Peter's [Catholic Church] almost immediately because of its location downtown in the middle of a very ethnically diverse neighborhood with many immigrant communities, across the street from Clark University, and connected to Assumption College. So we started different programs there to engage the students, and to be at the service of the immigrant community.

I've been here 13 years, what changes have I noticed [laughs]? Not much I think [laughs]. There have been more and more immigrants coming from Central American countries, a diversity of countries. I think the African community has grown quite a bit. At St. Peter's we have—it's the seat of African ministry, in the diocese of Worcester, and that's seen a great growth in the time that I've been here. A couple of years ago, we had a sister here from Rwanda who was studying at Assumption College and she was more involved with the African community, and I've really seen how it's grown over the years. So I think there's been an increase in the immigrant community in Worcester over the 13 years that I've been here.

Obviously the economic crisis now has affected everybody and impacted everybody. I know many people in the Main South neighborhood, where I work, have lost their jobs or have lost their homes. I think there's a real effort to keep people employed, but it's just getting harder and harder, and social services are being impacted at St. Peter's Church. We normally would serve 250 families at Thanksgiving and Christmas. Last Christmas and Thanksgiving that number rose to 480. So that's almost double the number of people who are coming to us for food assistance, heating bills, rent or medical bills, so clearly life is getting harder these days.

If there's something in the city I would change, I think I'd like to see an improvement in the public school system, in the quality of our educational offerings. I'd like to see better housing for people, better healthcare. It's a lot to put on the city, but I wish those problems could be addressed and, you know, food. There's hunger in the city. It's terrible to say it, but there are a lot of families that are hurting even with the basic issue of food. My work has been more with youth and immigrant people, but those are major issues: housing, health, education, also in terms of human rights for immigrants. I wish that could be improved through immigration reform.

I went to Catholic school all my life. I studied in the Philippines, so my grade school was done at the Maryknoll Sisters School, at the Maryknoll Grade School, and then I transferred to Assumption for high school, and I went to Assumption College in Manila for my undergraduate degree. Then I went to the Jesuit University in Manila for my master's degree in theology. I went to school at a time in my country when we were under the dictatorship of President Ferdinand Marcos. The Assumption sisters were being very true to the charism of our foundress, which was that our education and our faith had social consequences, that we couldn't be living in a situation of great poverty and of great injustice without somehow doing something with our education to make that better. And our faith also demanded that we do something to change the situation of the poor and of the unjust political system we were under. So I got very involved in social justice activities, and when I was in my senior year in college, I got arrested by the military and I was put under military arrest for four months. I had to stop my schooling—clearly [laughs] since I was under arrest. And then afterwards when I was released, I had one more semester to go in college and I graduated, but my family requested that I leave the country for a while because they never knew when I left the house in the morning, if I'd come back alive in the evening with the fear that I'd just be picked up by the military again.

So I left for the United States, and I worked in San Francisco for a year. But it was while I was in San Francisco, that I felt—I had been feeling the attraction to religious life for some time, but I never thought I could possibly be a nun, that I wasn't holy enough, I wasn't good enough, I wasn't—I just wasn't made out to be a nun. I wanted to have a family and I wanted to raise kids, and I had a boyfriend at the time and all, so I just didn't pay any attention to it. But it was while I was away from home and after the experience of the arrest, that I began to evaluate what really was important to me, and what were the deepest desires that I had, really, and I decided to face up to it and say, "Well I think God is calling me to be a sister whether I feel it or feel that I'm appropriate for it or not." And so I lived with the sisters in the United States for a couple of months just to observe their life. And then I felt it was more and more confirming my call to religious life. I returned to the Philippines and I entered there, but I guess the greatest challenge to my education was trying to put my education to work and to, to suffer, suffer in quotation marks, the consequences of that commitment to social responsibility, so that was it.

I'm so glad I made the choices that I did. I struggled over making them, but I am just so happy that I am a Religious of the Assumption, that I've become a sister with this congregation. The congregation has been really, really good to me and has given me so many beautiful experiences of life. Difficult things to say yes to—it wasn't easy to say yes to come to this country and be away from all that I love and know in the Philippines. It wasn't easy to say yes to being provincial superior of this congregation in the United States, but I have drawn so much life and beautiful experiences that I really am just grateful. I think that you know when we make our vows as religious, we make a vow of obedience and often it wasn't very clear to me where saying yes to something would bring me, but trusting in the will of God, and the love of God, and in the wisdom of my superiors, I said yes and really I couldn't have planned my life any better. I'm just grateful to be here and having had the experiences that I have had and continue to have.

Alison Graham
Age 32
Interviewed on March 3, 2011 by
Nicole Bell, Karalyn McCann, and
Erin McHugh of Assumption College
Overseen by Prof. Carl Keyes,
Assumption College

        I went to Gordon College,
and I studied in an honors program where I was able to

design my own major. I thought I was going to go into camp ministry and work with children in a camping setting, and then later realized that I had a huge passion for curriculum, and for teaching, and for working with students in that setting. So I got a job at a private Christian school. So basically graduated from college, got married, started working. I taught until Madeline was born, and my job basically stopped right when she was born because my world stopped. She was 11 weeks premature, and only a pound and a half when she was born. And so, I was done teaching, and became a mom of a very critically ill child.

Oh gosh, [the benefits of being a stay-at-home mom] they're innumerable. I definitely use my time well. We are busy. I've done a lot of volunteer work with the March of Dimes because of Madeline's premature birth. I tutor on the side. I've had as many as eight students at one time—right now only one. But that works for me because two kids can keep you really busy, so yeah, my priority has been to stay home, and it is the hardest job ever [laughs], and it tries me in ways that I never expected. I never thought myself an angry person before I became a mother [laughs], and it's just interesting because God has this way of teaching you, through children, and really refining your character [laughs].

The March of Dimes has a fundraising walk that happens annually. It's called the March for Babies. Our family has a family team and I am the team captain. We get together friends and family to raise money for March of Dimes. Each April is when we walk. I've also worked on a family team committee through March of Dimes to reach out to local families, who also walk at the Worcester walk, and to encourage them in their fundraising, and to answer any questions, logistical questions about the day, or anything else, and also to provide support. The last two years, I have actually worked for March of Dimes six months out of the year as a family team specialist, and that sort of took my volunteer role and made it a more statewide position, where I would work with six different walk sites, family teams that participate there were served by family team committees. And so, I was in charge of, basically, creating those family team committees, recruiting, training, and helping those volunteers do what I did in Worcester at six different walk sites across the state. And this year I just decided to turn the job offer down. Because of the revenue that was raised, and the increase of revenue due to family teams, the foundation wanted the job to be year-round. They wanted it to be more hours, double the hours that I was working, and so, that just doesn't fit into our family plan right now. I didn't want to be working that much on a year-round basis, but it was great. I mean, 10 and a half hours a week, six months out of the year, and I was able to do a lot of my work from home. While the children were napping or at school, I was able to work and do something meaningful in the community.

Some other volunteer work that I do is through my church. We go to Heritage Bible Chapel in Princeton, [Massachusetts], and we have recently opened a play gym for children zero to six, and so I have been spearheading that project with a committee of five other women that are also moms. Most of us are stay-at-home moms. We have opened a community play gym there with a bounce house and a big climby thing with two slides and a trampoline, and lots of space for kids to run around, and it's been a huge, huge success. We've had almost 70 kids every week over the course of three hours come to play. We're open weekly on Tuesday mornings from nine to noon, and that really, I mean, includes the recruitment of volunteers and staffing and all of the legwork, certainly I did not do all by myself. I also help facilitate a women's bible study at my church, and so, those things keep me really busy [laughs]. Never mind play dates and other things for the kids. So I feel like I use my time really well. [Laughs] As a Christian,

I want to be part of my local church, and want to just contribute any gifts and talents that I have to our community.

My college experience was phenomenal. But I don't feel myself pressured that I need to use my degree every moment of every day for the rest of my life. I have a huge value for family and, for me, I think my college education prepared me to be an educated woman who hopefully impacts society. I have skills that I can offer in various settings [laughs]. I learned how to learn. And so those things are very important, but just because [I have] my degree I don't necessarily think I have to be in the work force.

I think my value to family right now for this season trumps the education that I received. Do I believe that it was all for naught? Absolutely not. I learned how to be a good learner, and I learned so much that I am able to apply in various settings, but I think family is of the utmost importance and I think being there for children is also extraordinarily meaningful and fulfilling. As a parent, I'm helping to shape two little pieces of the next generation and to teach them to be responsible, and honest, and hardworking, and loving, and caring, and kind, and considerate, and compassionate. Those things don't necessarily get developed unless you're intentional about it. And so, I'm very intentional as a mom. For the next generation of women [laughs] to sum that up in a nutshell, I guess just to value things that are really important. Money, having money is important and nice, but it's not what life is all about. And being fulfilled certainly is important, to do something that is meaningful, but I think that as a mom and as a stay-at-home mom, there is meaning and worth that couldn't ever come from corporate America.

Kristin B. Waters
Age 54
Interviewed on October 13,
2006 by Alison L. Cantatore of
Worcester State University
Overseen by Prof. Lisa
Krissoff Boehm, Worcester
State University

I went to Bard College for my BA [Bachelor of Arts], University of Connecticut for my master's and my PhD [Doctor of Philosophy]. I'm a professor of philosophy at Worcester State College. I believe I started this job in 1999.

I earned a PhD in philosophy. I taught at Northern Illinois University in DeKalb, Illinois. That was my first job, full-time job as a philosophy professor. And then I was hired at Clark University, I taught there for a number of years. And then I went into administrative work, and helped to run the interdisciplinary program at the College of the Holy Cross, and then decided that I wanted a faculty position. And that's when I came to be here at Worcester State. I love this work; it's great. There's no better job than being in the classroom, teaching students, it's fantastic. I really think that my Worcester State students are the best; I really connect with them very well. I was instrumental in reviving the women's studies program here.

I'm of that generation when it was easy to be active politically. You rolled out of the bed in the dorm room and managed to stumble out the door of the dorm, there was a demonstration going on outside. Sometimes those of us of my generation who are critical of the younger generation for not being sufficiently active, we should remember that it really didn't take much effort on our part. But I was active in the Peace Movements in the 1970s. I came later to the Women's Movement, I think in part, because society is structured in such a way that it's difficult for young women to identify with the Women's Movement, because, at least for heterosexual women, there's always that fear of being labeled, and then of not being attractive. I mean, it tells you a lot about the mindset, the ideologies that we absorb, it's really too bad. I've marched in "Take Back the Night" marches; I've organized women's political events. Right now I'm co-chair of Daybreak, which is the Worcester organization to address issues of domestic violence.

[Laughs] My children are fantastic. I look at them, and I just marvel in wonder at how I got to be so fortunate as to have the wonderful, thoughtful, caring, smart, loving, successful kids that I have. So I get a lot of pleasure in that. I've had a lot of success; I've published a lot. I have a book that I'm very proud of called *Women and Men Political Theorists: Enlightened Conversations.* I've taught a course, political theory, for decades. And early on when I taught it, I taught it in a very standard way. I taught Hobbes, and Locke, and Marx, and Mill, and Burke and all the usual suspects, all of them male. And, at the same time, I was teaching women's studies courses, and it didn't take long for me to realize there was a disconnect between my women's studies teaching and my political theory teaching, and yet it actually was very difficult to get material—original material—by women writers in the modern period.

Mary Wollstonecraft was the one person who was taught. She wrote *A Vindication of the Rights of Woman* in 1792, and she might make an occasional appearance in these political theory courses. These political theory courses, by the way, are required of every undergraduate political science major throughout the country. So, you're talking about, literally, tens of thousands of people probably—I don't know if I'm exaggerating that—who are taking these political theory courses and they're only reading what men have to say about their experiences, their ideas, their concepts, their theories. And so I set about to do research to find women writers who are contemporaries of these male writers, and I found them. At first, I thought, "Oh well, there just weren't women writing in the seventeenth, eighteenth, and nineteenth centuries," but I was wrong about that. I found, for example, Mary Astell, who was a contemporary of John Locke, and she was his foremost-published critic when he was writing in the late seventeenth century. And her books are interesting, and they are about political theory, but they're also about women, the need for women's university education. She writes very illuminatingly about marriage, which is of course a political institution. So I created this textbook, which paired men and women authors: Mary Astell with John Locke, Mary Wollstonecraft's *A Vindication of the Rights of Woman* with Burke's *Reflections on the Revolution in France*, Wollstonecraft's *Vindication [of the Rights] of Woman* with Rousseau's political writing, and so on including Maria W. Stewart, an African-American woman who wrote about rights and liberties for Blacks in the 1830s. Anna Julia Cooper, another African-American woman, who wrote about education and other things. And this textbook, the aim of it, is to actually reconceive what we mean by political theory to include thought by woman and experiences by woman, and I'm very proud of it.

That book has been out since 2000. I have a new book. It's called, *Black Women's Intellectual Traditions: Speaking Their Minds*. My co-editor Carol Conaway and I put together a collection of 20 contemporary essays, current essays, really making the argument that there is a Black feminist theory that has existed for at least 200 years.

I think an important aspect of my story here in Worcester is the development of women's studies. I think about the development of women's studies at Clark [University], [College of the] Holy Cross, and here at Worcester State. This is a story that really should be told. I think the development of those programs were historically important. Clark had one of the very first women's studies programs in the country, and I was sort of in on the development of that. It was really exciting.

I wonder if, as I age, I will manage to achieve more peace and understanding. And part of that is just frustration with the world at large, which seems to be in such a terrible mess. And part of it is, sometimes I think I just know too much, I think, particularly about the suffering of women—about everybody suffering, but my focus has been women—and I find that unsettling. I know some people manage to be activists and not be—not let it disturb them too much. And also my personal life, I wonder what kind of peace I will find.

Melinda Boone
Age 53
Interviewed on February 28, 2013
by Andrew Lampi and Alina
Schmidt of Assumption College
Overseen by Prof. Carl Keyes,
Assumption College

Some of my hardest challenges [in my education] dealt with the issues of race. Through third grade, I attended segregated schools, all-Black schools. In fourth grade in Suffolk, Virginia, where I was raised, there was an opportunity for voluntary integration, because by fifth grade, it was going to be mandatory integration to integrate schools across the city. And so, my grandfather being progressive, suggested that I do the voluntary year of integration, where I went to a school that [was] primarily a White school—one of a handful of Black students in that school. And so there were challenges there, and then there were challenges the year of the mandatory integration. I'll never forget I got suspended three times in the same week in fifth grade, simply because the White teacher that I had—it was the first time working with Black kids, and it was obvious that she wasn't comfortable in the setting. And you know, my grandparents had taught me to be an advocate for what I believed in and for myself. And so we had a few challenges that week that resulted in me being sent home three times because I was an advocate for myself. That teacher didn't teach after that year, so I think I was the victor in that one.

And so the whole issue of integration, it worked well for us. But I remember there used to be an episode on Saturday Night Live called "Not Quite Ready for Prime Time Players." And I remember our high school's senior class skit was "Not Quite Ready for Class." And that was because we were the class that emerged through this integration, and we had a great relationship, our class members Black and White got along fine, but we talked about all of the things that we weren't quite ready for in education. I found myself all through high school still being an advocate, an honors student and doing well. I was one of a few students who was tapped when they wanted a Black student face or voice around the work and I used to say, "There are other talented students."

When I went off to the University of Illinois— here we are at 1981—this is how the dean of the school met us. We were told that there was this meeting. We all go into the department meeting thinking this was going to be for all new graduate students, and we looked around the room. Everyone in the room was Black. So then it dawned on us: "OK, this is a different type of meeting." The dean came in, head of the department, and welcomed us to the University of Illinois. He said, "But I need to let you know, not all the faculty share this sentiment. This is the first time that we've had this number of Blacks in our graduate program at the same time, and there are some faculty members who are afraid they may have to alter the program to accommodate you." And so, my girlfriend and I, as we left that meeting, looked at each other, and said,

"Oh gracious, what have we done here?" Once again, we found ourselves in the place of having to prove ourselves. And at that time, Illinois had a 5.0 system. For those of us in the audiology program, at the end of that first semester, three of us made 5.0s and two 4.8s. And so that began to help people understand we didn't come unprepared or underprepared.

There are three things that are so key for me. I said as I came to this community [as superintendent of Worcester Public Schools], three things that aren't negotiable for me in my life are my faith, my family, and my friends. And I am grounded by my faith, that's my anchor. And I also know that while that's my anchor for how I live my life, it's also my anchor to get through storms, if you will, and the challenges. And you talk about the difficulty of moving into Worcester. Worcester's a city that doesn't readily welcome folks who are not from here. And so, being the first woman, the first person of color, and the first person in 45 years hired for the superintendency from outside of the school system, some people said I came with bases loaded with three strikes and I said, "No, I came with bases loaded, the only place to go was a home run."

I firmly believe that God is the one who led me here, and He continues to provide me the wisdom to do what it is He would have me do for the children and for the school community at large. I had an initial three-year contract, and I'm on the first year of my next three-year contract. And, it was—it was tough. The first two and a half to three years were very difficult. Partly because of me being an outsider, and those who just wanted to push on that agenda of me not being committed or connected to this community. But I didn't let it deter me. And so it was my faith that has sustained me. It was my faith that has gotten me through the sudden loss of my high-school sweetheart. We had just celebrated our 22nd wedding anniversary, and he passed two weeks later. It's my faith that allowed me to understand that I had the best of both worlds when I had my parents, though I didn't spend most of my childhood with them directly, living under their roof. Being able to have a relationship with them that was nurtured by my grandparents who got me to where I am as an adult and yet to be able to, after my grandparents passed, to still have that strong and loving relationship with my parents. All of that is about my faith, so those things haven't shaken me. Life is about changes and challenges; those are things that are guaranteed in life. Your faith is what helps you figure out how you respond to those, so that you don't crash and burn, or crumble, and whatever else. As difficult as some of the journey has been, it's been a good journey, but my faith is what's guided me to that point.

Karen Jean White
Age 62
Interviewed on November 19, 2010 by Megan Chan and Samantha Minieri of Assumption College
Overseen by Prof. Arlene Guerrera, Assumption College

I've lived in other places for a short period of time, but basically my main residence has always been West Boylston, [MA]. I started teaching [dance] there when I was 13 at my house. And then I studied dance all the way along and in Boston and New York.

I was pretty much very fortunate to be brought up by parents who were available to us all the time. My father worked the night shift at a sheet metal company here in Worcester. He taught at a Worcester trade school as well. And my mother was—it was the old-fashioned days, my mother was home. She was there 24/7. You'd get home and she was right there saying how come that grade isn't a little bit higher. And she sewed, and cooked, and took care of everything, and she was a good financial planner. When I was 11, my Worcester tap teacher said there was nothing left for her to give me, to bring me to Boston. My father said, "Go ahead." So off we went to the Combat Zone [in Boston], where all the dance schools are. And my mother used to drive me down every Monday for four hours of classes. I had classes there as well as Berklee School. I had jazz piano there. I had classical piano from a teacher in Worcester

I applied to Worcester State College and I finished there in 1976, or '77, I don't even remember. I did student teaching in West Boylston and I put it toward an elementary education degree. So I do have that degree. But I didn't use it per se in the school.

[Dance] has been the focus and the great love of my life. It continues to be, only it's changed colors now. It's in a different venue because I don't dance as much now. I teach, but I don't dance as much. I don't demonstrate and move as much. I chose—when I was 13, I could see what this was going to be from my dance teacher who was married. I saw her expecting babies and still teaching. And her mother was good enough to help her raise the children. The father, her husband was working, too, so he wasn't available and I always felt, "Well, gee, I don't want to have a family like that because you have to pawn them off on someone else."

My dancers at the studio for years now they have to run around like crazy. Work, work, work, go pick up the kids. They're a cab driver pay, pay, pay, run, run, run and you know they all try to do everything with quality. And that's the whole key. They used to say, "Oh you can do everything you want." Well you can, but can you do it with quality? So for me, I always was delighted to see the kids come. I love children, I love working with them. So I thought well I think maybe I'll just concentrate on what I was doing.

The benefits are huge, huge. Being privileged enough to have what skills you have, your abilities, your opportunities and be able to take those in and hopefully turn them back into something in a good form and give back again. It's a tremendous, tremendous blessing, tremendous gift of living. Because the purpose when you get up in the morning, is why am I—what am I going to—what am I doing today is the purpose. And God only gives us one day at a time. So we don't need to worry about too much beyond that. Of course we have our plans, of course we have to focus to a degree, but it's like knowing who you are, and being able to learn who you are, and what it is that makes you unique. So the benefits of that are good. It's a lot of peace of mind eventually. You wrestle with a lot of things, of course, for many years. Life is one wrestling match after another.

I belong to Dance Masters of America, which is a certified dance teacher organization and I was very involved with that for years. I've been a member since 1972, and we would have master classes. We would take classes to extend our abilities and our knowledge once a month. And then another meeting would be the Dance Teachers Club of Boston. We do that every month, too. I've always had a great need to bring my dancers to the nursing home. We do nursing home shows and senior residences. We'd dance at veterans' homes or we'd dance up in Rutland, we danced on Shrewsbury Street for some politician's fundraiser, hospitals. Dance is a performing art, and if you don't perform, you don't get the experience and the confidence developing it. It's one of the greatest joys of all. I have students right through adult students who dance with me, little ones, and the parents of the little ones. Oh they love it, and this is great because to see the human interaction that goes on, the happiness, that's just key so it's really great. People who can't move and then they're watching other people that can, particularly the small ones that are so fresh and alive.

I think I'm very content and I'm very happy. You've got to keep looking over what makes you happy, what makes you tick. Do you see the good coming or do you feel good about it in your heart? And you've got to listen to your conscience, not what the society's telling you, because it's very confused out there.

Phyllis Estus
Age 74
Interviewed on October 22, 2007 by Eleis Brennan of College of the Holy Cross Overseen by Prof. Stephanie Yuhl of College of the Holy Cross

My husband was a graduate student at Duke [University], and we lived there for three years, and then moved to New York City where he was in graduate school and got his doctorate. I worked at that time at the national office of the Methodist Church. I worked with campus ministers across the United States.

That was really the beginning of a lot of activity in civil rights. My office, in my work with campus ministers, would sponsor a variety of things on campuses that dealt with civil rights, not only in the United States, but outside of it. We would arrange for people to speak from other countries at universities, and I did this for campuses over the entire United States. At Drew [University], by the time we were there, there were many things going on, such as the Martin Luther King marches. And also within that city and in New Jersey, there was the beginning of acknowledgement by the Blacks that they were not being treated equally. When we arrived, the barbershops wouldn't cut the hair of Blacks and it was like...what? And there was a lot of protesting by faculty members and students at Drew, and we were involved in that. Then we were involved very much in the Vietnam protests. As a result about 20 faculty members resigned from Drew because the president didn't like things that were going on, the president of Drew that is. Contracts were renewed, but no one got tenure, so there was a mass exodus. We were among those, so we came to Clark [University], and my husband taught for a few years at Clark before we came to Assumption [College]. Shortly after we came to Worcester, Eugene McCarthy was beginning his run for president and we supported him. Actually, we were quite involved in the Worcester Committee for McCarthy. My husband was the chair of that committee, and day and night we were working on that. [McCarthy] won in Massachusetts.

Then, around the early '80s, the Worcester Pushkin Sister City Project was formed and I became active in that organization. There had been an attempt to do that for a few years, because of the Cold War, to allow a person-to-person interchange with people from Russia. In this case, it was the way to start going up behind government to make a good impact. That was difficult because people in Worcester, particularly the newspaper, were very suspicious of any person or any group that had contact with Russia in any way, so we were all called Communists and things like that. Eventually we did have a sister city.

The Worcester Pushkin Sister Project was considered a great thing, we had many visitors from Pushkin both culturally and politically and also businesses. We also went there as a group—a large group of what was termed "artists" of various kinds. We had an art exhibit with crafts. We reciprocated and would have artists come here. During those years from the mid-'80s until 1998, when our Sister City Project merged with the International

Center of Worcester, we had lots of visitors from Pushkin and we sent lots of visitors there. The Performing Arts School sent musicians and orchestras. There were a couple of artists' visits. In that sense I was very involved in the Sister City Project. It took a lot of time; we merged with the International Center of Worcester in 1998. That involves having visitors from various countries. They are sent and approved by the State Department. They come here; we match them, with whatever their profession is, to someone here. We match them as a sort of internship here in their fields. I've been very involved with that, and that takes a lot of my time. I'm actually co-president this year. The other organization that I've been very involved in in Worcester since, I don't know '70 maybe around '70, first the Salisbury Singers, I was a member of that for about 13 years, and then I changed to the Worcester Chorus. I am still a member of the Worcester Chorus. I also belong to a women's group; its mission is to provide educational scholarships for college students. Those are my major organizations.

Carolyn Howe
Age 58
Interviewed on October 20, 2008
by Melissa Boisvert and Maria
Cerce of Assumption College
Overseen by Profs. Maryanne
Leone and Regina Edmonds,
Assumption College

I lived in Mexico when I was nine years old. We lived in a two-story house with four bedrooms and a balcony and a nice little gated area, and I had my nice little dog. Across the street there was a little adobe shack, adobe hut, where the watchman lived with his family who was watching over the building of a new church. My mom used to point out how even though they were very, very poor, the mother would come out and sweep the ground, and sweep the dirt floor, and sweep the dirt in front of the house, because she had pride in what she had, and that just really struck me. One time I was out on the balcony and I looked across the street, and I saw a little boy looking up at me, and he was about my age. And I mark that moment as the seminal moment in my realizing that this is not fair. It should not be this way, and I don't deserve this privilege and he doesn't deserve that poverty. So, I didn't really realize it at the time, but I kind of became a crusader for justice, and never felt insulted or personally attacked when people attacked the United States when I lived in Mexico. I thought, "They're not talking about me." I think that was very important.

And when I moved back to the United States, I entered ninth grade. I basically ended up skipping eighth grade. And we lived in a suburb of Denver. That was the same time that John F. Kennedy was killed. When I got home, I came into the house and I was just sobbing. [I] saw my mom dusting and she said, "Carolyn, what's the matter?" I said, "Now what's going to happen to the Negroes?" which was the politically correct term at that time for African-American people. And I guess I really saw John F. Kennedy as a savior. And halfway through that year we moved into Denver, kind of at my prodding and my mom's prodding. I thought that if we were professing a belief in integration, that we needed to live in an integrated neighborhood, not in the suburbs. So we moved into an integrated neighborhood and I went to middle school and made White friends and made Black friends, and lost some White friends when they saw that I had Black friends. It was a real taste of racism. I became very, very committed to becoming an anti-racist, which is a word I didn't know then, but I know now and I know that's what was happening to me.

My first job, out of my undergraduate education, was the bilingual teacher for migrant children in Greeley, Colorado, in one of the schools. And my goal was to make these kids feel proud of who they were, and to feel proud for speaking Spanish, because they didn't. And a moment of pride was that at a school board meeting, I stood up and said something about, "I'm a bilingual teacher, but I'm angry and I only get to work with migrant children not the other children who need bilingual education. The other bilingual teacher teaches Spanish as a second language, and doesn't even work with Chicano kids." I said something about tokenism, and the Latino community stood up, and looked back at me, and cheered. And the next day I was told there was no more money to maintain my position next year, so I should look for another job.

So I applied to [College of the] Holy Cross and got the job. I run a Latin American Studies program at Holy Cross. I really didn't want to move to New England. I had lots of second thoughts about coming, but one of the things that really drew me was hearing that there was a bilingual school here that my daughter could go to, Chandler Magnet School. I wanted her to have the bilingual experience that I'd had as a child.

My first major involvement [in the community] was becoming pretty much a full-time activist on the [Proposition] 2 ½ Override Campaign in 1991, which was a campaign to override a Massachusetts law that restricted cities from increasing taxes more than 2 ½ percent without a referendum vote to override that law. The part I worked for was for schools, to fund schools. I really immersed myself in the community through that effort. A lot of my motivation was to save bilingual education and the teachers who were committed to it.

And then in 1994, I heard something about this group that was getting together to celebrate the 150th anniversary of the First National Woman's Rights

Convention in the year 2000. I think my first event was going to a little rally, I think it was announcing the [Worcester] Women's History Project, and it was at City Hall. It became a quarter of a million dollar project that funded an original play, under the guidance of Karen Board Moran. After several chairs, I became chair of the program committee, and was clerk of the organization for a while and then became president the year leading up to the 150th anniversary of the First National Woman's Rights Convention. So I was president that year and the year following.

I think the 2 ½ Override Campaign and the Worcester Women's History Project helped me see a different side of Worcester, that there was a depth and a community that really cared. My personal feeling is that it's a great community to raise children in, or even to be an adult in, if you're reasonably well off. It's a really tough place if you're poor or below the median income. I think part of my awareness is recognizing that there is a large community of people in the upper middle class, who really care and are really trying to make this a better community, and there are a lot of people really suffering in this community.

And I think it also changed my view of the community when I learned about the tremendous history in abolitionism that came from this community. My heroine—I had trouble struggling between commitment to the Feminist Movement and commitment to the Civil Rights Movement, and I couldn't see how they meshed— is Abby Kelley Foster, who is from Worcester, who was one of the most important speakers and fundraisers and grass roots organizers of the abolitionist movement. She always linked the struggle for women's rights and racial equality, not just abolition but racial equality. She really believed in true equality of the races. To me, she is just a big inspiration.

When I was involved in the Worcester Women's History Project, most heavily for two years as president and for the years leading up to that and somewhat after that, I was *so* busy but I thought that in some ways that those were the most satisfying years of my life. I coauthored a play [*Yours for Humanity-Abby*] with Karen Board Moran, and that play has been performed by Lynne McKenney Lydick I don't know how many hundreds of times now, in schools and senior centers and libraries and all over the place and I think of that as one of my lasting legacies. I think that's what I wanted to do through my work with the Women's History Project was to let children know there is a history, this isn't a dump. [Worcester] used to be the center of activity for the whole Northeast region. It was a place people came to do all the things that needed to be done. They came for religious reasons, for temperance reasons, for abolitionists' reasons, for women's rights reasons. It was the center; it was the hub of activity and liveliness, and hold on to that. That's what I would like kids to get out of it. That and an oral history project and what we are continuing to do now.

Beatriz Patino
Age 34
Interviewed on
November 29, 2012
by Griffin
O'Donoghue and
Elena Losquadro of
Assumption College
Overseen by Profs.
Leslie Choquette and
Esteban Loustaunau, Assumption College

My mom is originally from Puerto Rico and my dad is from Mexico City, Mexico. While I was in high school, I was in a program called Upward Bound. It was affiliated with Rhode Island College. So, starting in tenth grade in high school, I spent every Saturday and every summer at Rhode Island College taking classes. And then for college, I went to Connecticut College, which is in New London, Connecticut. I graduated there in 2000. In 2001, I left for the Peace Corps and I was in Paraguay, South America, for two and a half years, so that's where I did my service. When I returned, I got a job at [College of the] Holy Cross, and then I came here to Assumption [College]. And at Assumption I went to school part time for my master's in counseling psychology and I graduated in 2008.

My first year at Connecticut College, it was a big culture shock. I had mostly grown up with people that looked like me. When I went to college, it was the first time—I was like, "I've never seen this many White people in my entire life." And this many people driving Volvos and Saabs. It was just a completely different culture and the high school I went to definitely didn't prepare me for college, so I found it really difficult. I probably lived at the—our version of the Academic Support Center. But I knew I was there for a reason, so I wanted to make sure to take advantage of that. My parents are divorced, so my mom raised me for most of her life. My father's in my life and has always been a part of my life, but financially my mom was the caretaker and provider. I'm actually the first person in my family to ever go to college.

I knew I wanted to go to Connecticut College. My Upward Bound counselor was like, "Well you have to apply other places," and I [asked], "Why?" and she [said], "Well you could not get in." I didn't even know they could say no. I had never met anyone who had even been to college. I didn't understand the process. So, my first year there I struggled.

I was really homesick, and then my mom lost her job. I had two older sisters, but they both got pregnant at

16, so they both started families pretty early and had other responsibilities. And then my brother was five years younger than me. So, I really felt like I had to step up, and it was a really hard decision, but my second semester freshman year I took off from college.

It was really hard for me to even concentrate [that first semester] when I knew my family was in need, and I felt like I could do something about it. I got two jobs and really was just trying to help out financially, and I was miserable and I was like, "My gosh, I really want to go back to school." Which really changed my perspective. When I got back on campus, I was eager and happy to be there and really valued the experience. So I kind of went at it totally differently when I finally went back. My dean said, "Your scholarship is only for four years, but it's time-sensitive. You have to graduate [in] May, 2000. So what that means is that semester you missed, you're going to have to make up somehow. It's either taking an extra class a semester, or taking summer courses. But it's not paid for." I worked while I was in college and so any money I made, I would spend on taking summer courses. So, I did it, which was [laughs] great, but it was really difficult. I worked at the Women's Center of New London, Connecticut, and I did some of their hotline work and newsletter work. That was more like my work-study job. And then my job job was I ran their after school program. I did that every day with the students in a transitional living shelter.

It was awesome. I just met such wonderful and empowering women [at the Women's Center]. It was a huge part of my experience there, and the work that I did because it was something I did every day. Not just from the women that worked there, but even the women that lived there. So listening to their stories and meeting their children—I really liked it because it really just opened my eyes to something different. When you're on a college campus [you can] get caught up in this bubble. I have all these papers and things to do. [The Women's Center] always set [me] back to reality, or even put things into perspective. I mean my doing a paper is not that bad, in comparison to hearing some of the stories of these women who had been abused for years and are trying to get their lives back together.

I really have no regrets. I think I've done the best with what I was given, and what I had, and what was put before me, and I've always tried to kind of challenge myself and try new things. Like going to college was one thing, but then even doing the Peace Corps. When I wanted to do the Peace Corps, my family kind of flipped out a little bit because—this is a direct quote from my family: "That's something only rich White kids do because they don't want to work."

I think financially my family expected me to finish college, and get a job, and help them. That was kind of the expectation and I think it kind of still is. I think they thought I was being very selfish. Even if I'm thinking, "People enter the Peace Corps, that sounds like the most unselfish thing," but to my family they just couldn't understand why I wanted to leave. I mean I didn't come home at all those two and half years. So, I think that was really difficult for them, but I really have no regrets.

One thing I've learned is the power of forgiveness and how important that is in life. So many people hold so many things in, and it really affects you, and eats at you, versus really doing anything for anyone else. It's really just so poisonous to yourself. So, I think forgiveness is really important. And just challenging yourself to try new things and not stopping yourself. The other thing I've learned is the power of vulnerability. I think it's really hard for people to open themselves up sometimes because I think so many times—I mean I could name a billion times in my life where I've been hurt by someone or something and I could have used that and been like, "Never again." But instead, I think I feel like you're never really going to experience the great things in life if you don't make yourself vulnerable. And open yourself up to some of those experiences because if you close yourself off, there's never really any opportunity to experience any of that. And it could be great and beautiful or it could not, but you'll never know.

Joan Phillip
Age 47
Interviewed on March 27, 2007 by Steve Wych of College of the Holy Cross
ASL Interpreters: Taylar Belsvick and Amanda Moyer of Northeastern University Overseen by Prof. Judy Freedman Fask, College of the Holy Cross

I have two sisters. All three of us are Deaf. My father is Deaf as well as one of his sisters. I was born here in Worcester as were my sisters, so the three of us grew up here, but we went to school in Connecticut [American School for the Deaf]. And we had a lot of deaf friends there. It was really easy to socialize and interact with other Deaf people there at school. But over the summer a lot of people went home. The school was in Connecticut and most of my friends lived there, but my sisters and I lived in Massachusetts so we came back here and pretty much it was just the three of us for the summer together. When my sisters went to college, I was even more alone. I liked being at school more. It was more of a safe environment for me. Everyone had the same method of communication, and it was a lot easier to interact with other people.

Every year for Christmas Eve we would gather at Nana's house, the whole family would get together. The non-deaf family would get there and be hanging out, socializing, and talking. When the Deaf family members would arrive we'd do our greetings, say hello, and then migrate to a different room in the house. And for most of the night we'd stay in those separate rooms, we didn't socialize very often. It was more comfortable for us to stay in those separated groups for the sake of communication. Occasionally, a family member would go back and forth between the groups, but it didn't last very long. It just wasn't as comfortable.

It was not easy. I remember it always being a struggle to try to communicate. If it was one on one, we could try to communicate by writing. It was a little bit easier, but as soon as the group got big, and the kids were playing together, if I tried to join, I felt left out. Everyone would be talking, and to try to keep up with communication and follow what was going on was hard. They would also make fun of me. For example, they would say, "Say this word," maybe the word cat, "Say the word cat." I would try, and I would speak, and I would try to say the word cat, and they would make fun of me. They thought I sounded funny. The way that I said it was different from them. After that experience, I stopped using my voice. I wasn't comfortable speaking. The only time I feel comfortable using my voice is with my animals, when I'm at home with my pets. My dog or cat, I don't care about speaking with them because I know they won't make fun of me.

Growing up, my father was a huge inspiration to me and a huge role model. My father was very involved in the Worcester Deaf Club, and he was a great motivator for Deaf people in the area. He was always supportive of Deaf people getting together and socializing, for example, in sports or other leadership roles. He was also a very big supporter of hearing people learning sign language. He thought it was a great idea for hearing people to learn sign language, and to understand Deaf culture and how Deaf people communicate. And I'd always watch my father's leadership and admire that.

Back when I was growing up, there were no services for Deaf [people]. And when Deaf people needed help, where did they go? They came to our home. I remember many times sitting at the dinner table, and our doorbell light would go off to signify that there was someone at the door. And my dad would answer the door, and there'd be a Deaf person who needed help. My dad would invite them in, offer them some dinner, and they would usually go sit in the living room. My dad would finish dinner with us, and then go into the living room where they would discuss the person's problem. And my dad would try to help in whatever way he knew possible. And that was really internalized. His leadership skills were a huge inspiration to me. And now I'm really involved in the Worcester Deaf Club. I love the Worcester Deaf Club! And we're celebrating our 60th anniversary this year, and it's a great feat because many Deaf clubs have been closed all over the nation. And I'm trying to keep his dream alive through the Worcester Deaf Club and through my involvement in the Deaf community.

I've worked [at the Center for Living and Working] for 22 years now. Twenty-two years, wow! When I started that job, I never thought I would last that long. I came in as a part-time position and I worked for about 12 hours a week. I [advanced] in the company, and I [became] the director of the Deaf and Hard of Hearing Independent [Living] Program. Looking back, that desire to support and motivate Deaf [people] relates to my dad and how he loved to support Deaf people, and encourage Deaf people, and I really love my job. Every year I see the program grow. And Deaf people succeed and become more independent. And the job is very based on the individual client's needs, and so I like that and I also like living in Worcester.

I work there to teach clients to be more independent and to teach them their rights. For example, we teach a lot of clients their rights for an interpreter. And we also teach them how to set up their home for a safe environment. For example, how you set up doorbells that have flashing lights, and alarms that have flashing lights. We also help people teach landlords [that it is their] responsibility [to provide adaptive] equipment [for Deaf tenants].

I understand the hardship that non-deaf parents go through when they have a deaf child. With their history of spoken language in the household, it's hard to have a kid with different communication needs, and I understand the despair. But I think it's important for parents to try to consider all the possibilities and what the options are for their child, what resources they can tap into for their child. Most parents when they have a deaf child, the first person to give them advice is their doctor. And most of the advice they give is to not use sign language, and to use hearing aids, or maybe even to get a cochlear implant. But parents should really be aware of all the options that they have. They should go meet Deaf community members [to] see what our lives are like. Go and observe different schools, mainstream and deaf school settings. And keep an open mind to the possibilities. They can maybe visit parents, who have deaf children, and see what their experiences were like raising a deaf child. A lot of parents get so afraid when they find out they have a deaf child, their first instinct is to try to make them like them and either use hearing aids or implant them. But a lot of times those children struggle with their implants or with their hearing aids. I understand the heartache, but it's important for parents to keep an open mind. I'm very proud of my accomplishments related to my work and with the Deaf community and in Deaf programs.

Ann Lisi
Age 45
Interviewed on November 1,
2005 by Andrea Pesantez of
Worcester State University
Overseen by Prof. Lisa Boehm,
Worcester State University

When I was 14, I took a job in the summer. I was in the cornfield in Wisconsin detasseling corn. I have not stopped working since then. I left Wisconsin after graduating from university when I was 22 years old, and I did have a friend who had moved to Massachusetts, so I just came by myself. I had no job. I had no idea really of what I was going to do except look for a job, and I had a little bit of money saved up from my waitressing through college. I had $1,000, I had a stereo, I had a bicycle, and I had some clothes. That's all I brought with me. And I asked someone from my work to give me a ride, and he and his wife drove me across from Wisconsin to Massachusetts.

Actually, first I came to Salem, Massachusetts. Then after about five or six years working, I got involved in fundraising and nonprofit management, and then came to Worcester. Each job built on something for the next job. I didn't go to school to be in a foundation, but my college education certainly gave me skills in writing, reading, communicating, and critical thinking. Also, the experience of being in college made you think about the world and its problems. And for me, I took it as a time to reflect on where I fit in. What I saw was a need to solve problems. When I came east I applied for a job at a battered women's program. It was called Help for Abused Women and their Children, and actually I went in there to see if I could be a volunteer in a hotline while I was waitressing. They actually had a job opening for coordinator of volunteers. I really learned how a small organization with lots of volunteers was helping all these women make safety plans. We would help them figure out a plan for becoming safe, and helping their kids become safe.

I was learning how to organize, and reach out to new people to volunteer, and do public relations with the newspaper, and conduct training programs. And I really learned a lot about how the community tries to solve a problem, and then that job really led to some other jobs that I had. But I would say that it is because I just keep working really hard, and I was very fortunate, I had mentors. My boss took me with her when she went to another job in a fundraising office of a children's museum, so I was her assistant. I got to learn about membership campaigns and capital campaigns, serving donors and members at the children's museum. And then again because of people that I knew and my network, another mentor showed me about a job that she needed to fill at a Boston foundation, and so I think I just learned to be open to people seeing my talents and trust that they will support me if I didn't know things.

I learned on the job and I learned about fundraising and membership from my boss. By the time I came to Worcester, I had some background that this organization needed, and got the job as the program officer. And then three years into that, my director left and so this foundation was without a leader, and the board asked me to serve in that role while they searched for an executive. I decided I wanted to apply for that position as well. In 1992 I was appointed the executive director at the Greater Worcester Community Foundation.

I always have [volunteered] and I would say that's part of the training and part of the reason why I'm in the field of nonprofits [in] a paid position now. I had to get a volunteer job for confirmation class and I signed up to be a telephone reassurance volunteer. Every day I telephoned a lady, an elderly woman who was living alone. Her name was Ellen and I would call her every day at 4:30 no matter what I was doing. I could be off with my boyfriend on my bike and I'd say, "We have to get to a phone." [I'd] phone her and just say, "What did you have for lunch? How was your day? How's your neighbor, how's he doing?" She would just tell me the news of her day. I did that for six years, so that was probably my most long-term volunteer involvement. And I volunteer by serving on boards because that's the best way I feel that I could help. Last spring I volunteered at Citizen School. So every Thursday I went to Worcester East Middle School, and taught a class with the kids after school. I had a group of about 10 middle-school-aged kids. It was really fun.

My particular interests are so wide and so varied that being at the Community Foundation is a really good way to serve. The foundation's mission is to enhance the community through all sorts of nonprofit support, and so groups that you might think of like the Food Bank, or the Oak Hill Community Corporation, or the New England Assistance Dog Program, Joy of Music Program, organizations out there that are providing services and all sorts of interesting things for people of all ages. We provide money for them and help them evaluate their successes, so I can't really think of something so stimulating and exciting, because it covers so much.

I think Worcester has shaped me in my professional role. It gave me the chance to form my leadership abilities because of the position that I hold at the Community Foundation. And I hope that in my 15 or 16 years here I helped shape the Community Foundation, to grow it and make it a respectable organization—which it certainly was when I joined it, but to enhance all of that. And that by growing the foundation, by bringing in more gifts and more donors, doing creative things with our grant money, I hope that I've had an impact directly on Worcester through the grants that we've made and through the leadership that we provide.

Hilda Ramírez
Age 47
Interviewed in Spanish on March 31, 2011 by Jonathan
Scully, Ysander Figueroa, Frank Flynn of Assumption
College
Translated from Spanish to English by Stephanie Chery,
Bonnie Srubas, Megan Libbey of Assumption College
Overseen by Profs. Maryanne Leone and Esteban
Loustaunau, Assumption College

I grew up in a small town in the Dominican Republic and then I moved to New York, a very big city. A transition from a small town to a big city is always difficult for a child, I was 10 years old. I was so scared. New schools, new friends, and adapting—so it was quite intimidating. I attended Lesley University where I studied business administration. And then I attended Harvard [University] where I studied education—administration and education.

I think I know how to live in two cultures. I do not live in one or the other but in both. I have a new identity as a Latina American. You do not hold back on your culture, nor [do] you accept the other. You learn to live in the two cultures. I consider myself bicultural, so that's a new identity.

I respect living in this country, I love the principles of this country, and that's why I live here. I consider a lot of the elements of this country to be really part of who I am, too. And so I am very comfortable with it because I'm in an environment where that's celebrated constantly. We eat Latino food at home a lot, and we listen to Latino music and sometimes it is an overdose, and it is! And it's a criticism sometimes because we live it so much and that's why it has been so hard. And I'll say it in English and then I can tell you in Spanish because it will be a hard thing for me because it's more of a political side of me—that is why it is so difficult [for] schools in dealing with kids and Latino kids because there is a certain way to educate in the American culture, and Latino kids come with a lot of that passion and a lot of that native language and all of that. So, it is hard to balance the two, when you are trying to shape a mind, and so that is part of the criticism and the challenge at the same time.

I am very proud to be a Latina. That comes from my parents celebrating what it means to be Latina, the food, the religion, the music. It is something you grow up knowing who you are, having an appropriate identity that celebrates who you are. Sometimes the challenge is that many people do not understand why Latinos are so Latino. Well, because we love who we are, right? America offers many great things that we adopt. So, we live with two identities.

I work at the Worcester Youth Center. My title is the executive director and my responsibilities are to make sure that we have plenty of resources, that the facility is running well, that all the youth are developing positively towards the mission here at the Center, to make sure we have sufficient resources to do everything.

One thing we try to do here for the youth is to emphasize the importance of education. That's job number one. They need to turn around and find their passion in education. At some point, that link was broken in all of them. There are not jobs if you do not have the skills. Then, the first thing we try to do is to bring them here, even if all they do is play basketball or anything else, [then] it is talking about plans for the future, for education and a job. We try to guide them in that direction.

For me it is because I see the way of the urban communities, the neighborhoods sometimes are bad, there are many gangs, there is a lot of violent activity, all of it. What can they hope for in that community? So I do not want to say that it's because you are poor that you cannot aspire to be something better. For me, education is a way to leave poverty behind.

I grew up in a similar neighborhood and I also completed my education. I believe that the difference is what happens at home. If you do not have two parents who would tell you, "This is what you have to do," and who would guide you, then your path is broken. Many of our youth, unfortunately, do not have parents; live in foster homes, where perhaps they do not understand who they are. It's difficult for a young person. So there should be lots of help, not just for Latino kids, but for whichever student needs it.

Here, in the Youth Center, the positive is that every day you're seeing all these kids and making something better. For example, in this room, the GEDs [General Equivalency Diplomas], that are about to finish, you know every kid and say, "OK, this kid has finished here, so he can go to college, he can work, he can do something positive." So, daily we're seeing the results of our work. So, it's really a good experience because that's what I want to do with my life to make sure that we're making a difference, for, hopefully, the kids who don't have these opportunities. The negative sometimes is that, for example, here in this city, they always associate Latino and African-American kids, or whatever, "Oh, these are gang members. Come on. We don't want to see them, we don't want them." So, in one way or the other, it's negative, because every kid has his story. Perhaps they make mistakes, but they're human beings, and you have to help them. I know this, but at times, it's difficult for them, to leave this mix. That if you look a certain way, then you are doing something negative. That sometimes is the bad. But we work every day to make it better. The staff that I try to hire are people that love what they're doing, that are in this because they understand the youth, because they know that to make a difference, they have to give of themselves, right? So there's not a lot of turnover.

It's a stressful job. Why? Because you're constantly trying to change behaviors, right? So they're not bad kids, you just have to redirect behavior all the time. In here, you're modeling what you want to see all the time so, "I want good language, I want good behavior, we need to push, we need to push you. What are you doing now?" It's like a parent of 700 kids. And so, it's a lot of work. Yes, they are improving their lives. Sometimes we don't need to meddle too much. We give them options so that they can make their own choices. We are not here to decide what they need to do, but to guide them in the right path.

Mimoza Koshi
Age 44
Interviewed on November 5, 2013 by Lucelis Perez and Nguyen Tran of Assumption College
Overseen by Profs. Leslie Choquette and Alison Meyer, Assumption College

I was born in 1969 in Albania. My parents still live in Albania. I often talk with them through Skype. We came to America, June 1999. And we came here to Worcester, Massachusetts. We came to U.S. [United States] through a program, DV [Diversity Visa]. It's something that you get selected to work in U.S. I remember when I came here, there was a different environment. It took me a long time to adjust, long time. I had to come, and to face a different culture, different way of living. When I moved here, I spoke no English.

It was a long way for me, but always I see myself as [having a] great opportunity to come here. We believe as a family in education, and me and my husband, we went to night school to learn English. Then continue to work two jobs and keep a family. My husband graduated from Worcester State University with master's degree in biotechnology and I received bachelor's degree from Assumption College. I graduated 2010 for business administration. I really see that as great accomplishment. Something that I can show to my kids that they can do better than I did.

When I arrived here, I had no family, I had language barrier, I didn't know any English. Yes, there were a lot of challenges—I would say the adjusting to the new country, new environment, culture. I had to learn about different history. I have to learn about how to interact with the different cultures and learn from that kind—value and respect them, too. So it's a great adjustment on this culture. America is melting pot, so we're all from different countries. We got to respect, but still preserve the culture, too. I had difficulty coming up through here, through now. The barrier on the language was a big one. I'm beginning to understand the basics, but all of those challenges were overcome by my hard work and my persistence that I have.

Besides my mother language that is Albanian, now I am in English, of course [laughs]. But I speak moderate Spanish and write. I do have much interaction with Spanish-speaking customers, and it does give me enjoyment where I am able to not only serve them, but help them on their language. I have met different immigrants here that they come recently from Bhutan, Nepal, or from Iraq. On those languages, I've tried to learn what is essential for communication for banking, and greetings, and, being immigrant and not knowing the language and being in environment and someone tells you something in your language, it's very helpful for them. They see someone who is someone there that cares for them. Always I have in the back of my mind to try to help and be open-minded, to learn. I had taken a Russian language for eight years back home, but I haven't really practiced and if you don't use it, you lose it, but always I'm open to learn more languages and to interact. It's eye opening. [The] more you talk with the different cultures, more you get into learning about values, about tradition, about the food, more you learn from it, more you adjust, more you get.

I work as a banker. I work for Santander Bank. I have been working for them for 12 years. And right now I get promoted as a branch manager. I have started from teller, go up to lead teller, to supervisor, to teller manager. I have done personal banking, and now I get promoted to the branch manager.

When first I came here, then I spoke no English. I did work at the coffee shop and I work at this restaurant food court, and one of the restaurants close down and I wasn't employed for one month. Even though I was working, always I was looking for a way to improve myself to find a better job, to find a better education. Always I was on a search for the jobs, and one day I go to the bank. I was doing my banking, and I was asking, always trying to connect with the woman. So I connect with people, then ask questions. I'd ask if they had opening, and they told me that there is some opening. They got the manager to talk with me. So they allowed me to apply, and they gave me the interview. So I was able to pass those, and I was happy and thanked them for the opportunity they gave me. It's only one month that I wasn't employed, but always I got employed further, always I was applying, applying, and looking to find connections. Finding connections, networking with other women where they working, to see opportunities opening, job openings, and to match my skills and my education, was what I was looking for.

And really I am proud of what I've done so far and always, as I told you, I meet a lot of people and a lot from different countries. And in Worcester we see a lot of newcomers who are immigrants from different countries, and I'm always trying to talk to those women, how they can become someone in this country. They have this opportunity. That's how I see it.

Lisa Connelly Cook
Age 51
Interviewed on October
17, 2012 by Carissa
Couture and Chelsea
Gamboa of
Assumption College
Overseen by Profs.
Leslie Choquette and
Esteban Loustaunau,
Assumption College

I think the history of Worcester makes it so distinctive. Worcester is historically a hard-working town. It's been a place that has attracted entrepreneurs, workers, people with ideas, and people with commitment to social justice. And the legacy of those initiatives and successes is still around in the community in a lot of ways.

I guess the main or the biggest way [I've been involved with community volunteer work] would be with the Worcester Women's History Project, and founding that organization and at least for the early years being very, very involved with that. And being a founding president and organizing the celebration of the 150th year anniversary [of the First National Woman's Rights Convention held in Worcester in 1850] and bringing that information to the public, and working with other people who are interested in it, too. [I was committed to] organize public awareness and do fundraising and organize not just that Women 2000 celebration, but the organization itself, and bring it to life, basically as part of the community.

I was at Clark [University] and I was taking a class on women in the law, and we were reading a book by Eleanor Flexner called *A Century of Struggle*, and I read this section about Worcester and the 1850 convention, and was surprised I had never heard of that before. And it had just occurred to me that—at that time it was like 1992—that

2000 would be the 150th year anniversary and it was only a few years away, and wouldn't it be cool to do something about it! And that was sort of the beginning—thought of it, but I really didn't know anything about it. I didn't know anything about the Women's Movement from that time, or Worcester, or Abby Kelley [Foster], or any of these things.

And so then I saw that there was going to be a talk at Abby's House about Abby Kelly Foster, and I went to that talk and met Annette Rafferty who runs Abby's House, and Elaine Lamoreaux who was also working with her in that, and Al Southwick who was a local historian. I proposed the idea to Annette Rafferty. And she thought it was a good idea. Then I went to another event there later, and met Angela Dorenkamp and told her and she was really supportive. She had actually written an article that was published in the newspaper about the Seneca Falls Convention, and so I had read that and I was like, "Oh you know I have read your article and I would really like to do something like that about the 1850 convention." I ended up going to the YWCA to look for a space to have a little meeting, and from there met Linda Cavaioli who was totally enthusiastic about it. And she had seen the article that I had published in the paper, and from there we just started talking to people and there was so much interest in it. Right away people were like, "I never heard of that! That sounds like a good idea! I want to do it." So many people just wanted to jump on and get involved. Yeah, it was a lot of energy.

I think [we] called awareness to the history in Worcester, [by] actually having this celebration, and commissioning a playwright to create the reenactment [entitled *Angels and Infidels*]. We did this dramatization of the original event. Well, the original event was two days long, but Louisa Burns-Bisogno did this dramatization where she pulled what was known [of] what had happened, and what was said in the various newspaper articles [about the 1850 First Woman's Rights Convention] into a 90-

minute play. I think there was a dress rehearsal that was open to Worcester public schools, but there were three formal productions of it.

I think that in terms of Worcester, many women did take an active interest in the community, did give their time, and did try to make things better—make things better in their community and in their world. They did make an effort, and so many women are forgotten.

Gladys Rodríguez-Parker
Age 53
Interviewed in Spanish on
March 18, 2011 by Teresa
Budd and Katelyn Phaup of
Assumption College
Translated from Spanish to
English by Fitore Giemnica,
Jenny Stone and Nancy
McAdam of Assumption
College
Overseen by Profs. Maryanne
Leone and Esteban
Loustaunau, Assumption
College

I was raised on a farm until I was 12 years old. And when I was growing up I had no [running] water. We had to go get water and carry it up on our heads. And I didn't have electricity. The day before we left for the United States, the first electricity pole was installed in the village where I came from.

I have seven brothers. I am the only girl. I am the third and, of course, I had to take care of five of them because in the Hispanic community, especially the Puerto Rican community, women are in charge, even as a child, of washing, ironing, doing all you have to do at home.

As a child, there was never money. I used to go to school without shoes. We had other families who lived here in the United States who would send us clothes. And that's how we went through life. But to have money, if one didn't work one didn't have it, but we never had it.

I went to high school at North High School. My last year I got pregnant. I had a child during my senior year of school, and I thought I would never go to school again because my life was over now that I had my son. I spent some time thinking that there wasn't much hope for my future. But there was one person we had met while living in Plumley Village, which was a project here in Worcester, and I thankfully had the good fortune of meeting this lady who continues to be a good friend of ours. And she was my mentor. She advised me to attend a program at UMass Amherst [the University of Massachusetts at Amherst] where they were looking for students like me, experiencing a great deal of poverty who had promise, but not opportunities because of money, etc. We went to UMass. I loved it! And she said, "Gladys, you can come here and you can bring your son. There is no reason why you can't continue studying." And in 1975 I, along with my baby who was six months in August, moved to UMass. I attended college there for three years because I loved the place, I loved the school, I got involved in all the school organizations, met people from around the world. But after three years I could no longer do it, because of my son, because of everything, because of all the problems you have in college. I said to myself, "Let me go back to Worcester." I returned, I started working, but then I had a desire to finish my studies. Meanwhile I had my second child and in '84, nine years after I started at UMass, I graduated from Worcester State College with my bachelor's in history and political science.

A Puerto Rican is a person who is very friendly; a Puerto Rican is a person who—if you get the chance to go to Puerto Rico one day, you will see, how would you say "hospitable"? You will see that you will be treated as very special. The treatment that a Puerto Rican gives to others is very different. For example, we had a meeting at 12. Then this girl got here today. There are people in the Anglo community, the business community, that if they have an appointment at 12, that's all that they focus on. If this lady had a problem, or whatever it is, for me, it is my personal duty is to help this lady. That's a cultural distinction that people do not understand. Sometimes I get out of here and go to a meeting at City Hall, and I meet a lady or a gentleman or someone who needs help. I'm not going to let them remain in the street! My duty as a person, my duty as a Puerto Rican, is to find a way to resolve something in this instant and be late to the meeting. It doesn't matter whether everything is going well at this meeting, but they see it as a "signal" that one is not interested, that one is not being professional, that one is not respecting the way things are done here. This is something different that's a bit of an example of our culture.

When my boss, [U.S. Congressman Jim McGovern], won his office I was working in a program at UMass [Medical School]. My work was to search for students to go to medical school who were minority students because in medical schools we do not have the amount of minorities we needed. Before that I had participated in two or three events with my boss. But my participation in politics was always as an activist, from the outside. Therefore, when my current boss was elected, they called me—they caught me by surprise. And when they say, "You do not know what you're getting into," it's very true! Because [as senior district representative for United States Congressman Jim McGovern I have] a position that is super, super—the most important thing I have ever done in my life, I believe, apart from raising my children. It has been what I've been doing for the last 14 years with a person who—he is a person who lives what he represents and I am the same way. If my boss was a person that I did not get along with or if I did not believe in this person, I wouldn't be here.

There isn't a typical day here. Here, every day, every hour, there is something different going on. Sometimes on a Friday afternoon we have received calls from parents who are very anxious because their children who are in Nicaragua, or went to Spain or Europe and went on a trip with their friends and their family didn't hear from them for two or three days. It can also happen that a person arrives here with children because they have been evicted, their family has left them abandoned, they don't have a place to go—one has to act rapidly. So many of the problems that we face happen to be social, related to human services. Here, we help people. But when a person arrives at the office of a congressman, it's because that person has already heard "no" in many other places. That person is so, so frustrated, unaware of what else to do and that's why that person is now here. We, on a typical day, can have people protesting against the Iraq War and Afghanistan just outside of our office, or a group of people who are opposed to something that our boss is saying in Washington. A lot of what we are working on now is with refugees from Iraq, refugees from Africa. These are people who have been divided. They have family in their countries and are trying to reunify with the family here.

For me, being a Latina is more and more special every day. To be Puerto Rican is—well, for me [it] is everything. Now to be a Latina means that I am part of a family, of a larger family beyond the Puerto Rican community. And for me, it is a pleasure when I meet women from all of Latin America who are committed to the improvement of our people. And in the most recent census, the numbers are going to indicate that the Latino community keeps on growing. The majority of the Latino community are women, and I believe that this is a very important aspect for us.   To be a Latina also brings a set of problems because when one is a Latina and a strong person, sometimes this represents many problems.   Puerto Rican women excel and are known to have strong personalities. Culturally, what we Latinas have in common with other women—with Anglo-Saxon women—is that even now the system still is being controlled by men, and the social context in which we live is just the same.   We, as women, still need to work, to make the effort, and not to compete against each other in order to arrive at the table where decisions are taken.   Much of the reason why I am still in this office is because I've always realized that if one is not seated at the decision-making table, when the resources arrive, these resources are not really going to be made available to the people who most need them.   This is because the people with the resources have not met someone who understands the real problems that are out there.   For example, in this office, I am the only person who had children out of wedlock.   I am the first person that has been raised as I was raised.   The only person who has been on welfare, who depended on food stamps. When these issues are discussed I can say, "No, no, no that is not how things really are."

Konstantina Lukes
Interviewed on November 14, 2012 by Dominic Costanzo and Jordan Tofalo of Assumption College
Overseen by Profs. Leslie Choquette and Esteban Loustaunau, Assumption College

I actually decided to go into politics and law school when my father introduced me to the mayor at age eight or nine. I probably should include that my parents came from Albania, and it was a country that was governed by a dictator, and citizens were not allowed to come or go out of the country. The letters we received from our relatives were redacted, so there was always some government official who was reading the mail before it left, and read the mail when it came in, and censored parts. And my godfather, who was in this country, decided that he missed his family, so went back. When he lived in Albania, he realized that it was too oppressive. When he tried to leave, they threw him in jail as a political prisoner. There was that kind of abusive political power that made me think that we should do something about it.

I ran for [Worcester] School Committee in 1979. I was elected my first time out, served in 1980, and a two-year break so it's about 30 years. [Served on the Worcester City Council since 1990 and first elected female mayor of Worcester, MA.] Don't know what the impact is. How do you know whether there is one person where you made a difference? I'm told I am an independent voice; I'm told that I stopped abuses from occurring or escalating.

I've been a registered Democrat all my life; I became a Democrat when I was in college. That party really attacked the status quo and was active in civil rights. It has strayed from the party that I knew when I registered. And now instead of helping the oppressed, it is the oppressor, and one party rules in Massachusetts. I think it is detrimental to the state. There are no checks and balances because the Republican Party is so weak, and so the [last] election reflected that. I never thought the Republicans were going to win that election. So that was irrelevant and we are in Massachusetts. Massachusetts was going to vote overwhelmingly for the Democratic candidate. The only thing I was disturbed at was that Scott Brown was unable to succeed in his election.

Being a candidate and being a public servant are two different jobs. A candidate has to be a public relations person, and the product you're selling is yourself. One of the unfortunate rules of politics is, as I've learned, that you can say anything when you're campaigning, and it doesn't have to be true. So, you have a situation like a Harry Reid saying that Mitt Romney hadn't paid taxes in 10 years, totally untrue, but some people believed it. And there are no sanctions for saying those kinds of untruths because the Supreme Court *Times* case says everything's fair game unless there's malice attached to it, and it's difficult to prove malice. So, basically it's a free for all. And as a campaigner, if you don't understand you will be the subject of that—to those kinds of attacks—you're not going to be able to function. And now we have technology as part of the dynamics. Bloggers can get on, be anonymous, and say the most vile, vicious, malicious things about the candidate—or a public servant—and be able to repeat it over and over again. I had one person who's been doing that to me for the past 10 years. Calls up the radio stations, goes on blogging, a vile person, but he gains stature by attacking me.

But you have to understand that once you throw your name into the political arena, you're public property, and if you don't understand that, and can't accept it, get a nice 9 to 5 job. So public service means another thing other than promoting yourself, you have to know how to solve problems and meet the needs of your constituents. That doesn't mean you're not always campaigning, but it means that you have to shift your attention away from headline grabbing. Some politicians are always going to be headline grabbing. The unfortunate truth is that if you don't, other people will do it, and they will steal your ideas, so it's a constant dilemma.

When I made up my mind to go to law school, I had my guidance counselor in high school tell me it was not a good idea. The associate dean at UConn [University of Connecticut] told me I was taking up a spot that was more appropriate for a male to be in. I was going to get married, and have children, and wouldn't practice anyway. And when I went to look for a job, recruiters basically said the same thing. So it was constant fighting against stereotypes. First thing I did when I came to Worcester, was sue the city. I sued the registrar of elections on behalf of a woman because the registrar would not allow her to vote unless she used her married name. And there was no requirement in all 50 states that a woman, just because she was married, had to change her name. And so that was my first experience in Worcester. I had joined the ACLU [American Civil Liberties Union] legal panel, and then I became the director of ACLU, which was a relatively short period of time, but about two years because then I decided to run for office on the School Committee. I also initiated the Status of Women Advisory Committee with the city manager's office in Worcester. [I was] the first chair. I think it was just a battle to deal with those stereotypes. A woman, in order to prove herself, had to think twice as hard as a man. You have to keep plugging away at people and be persistent.

Robyn Kennedy
Age 32
Interviewed on October 22, 2013 by
Stacia Tympanic and Kylie Zurn of
Assumption College
Overseen by Profs. Leslie
Choquette and Allison Meyer,
Assumption College

Politically speaking, I think women have not [historically] had a great experience. There are not a lot of women in politics in Worcester, particularly not in local government. Well now that I say it, there are two women in the state delegation, but I think Worcester, for a very long time, has been thought of as the old boys' network. I think a lot of that has changed. I think more recently elected officials, especially I guess male elected officials, have been a lot better about engaging women, especially engaging young women, and getting them involved, and supporting female candidates. So, I think it's changing, but I think that is something that certainly sticks out for a woman's experience in the city.

I don't know that it's necessarily even that women have stayed away from it, more than there just hadn't been a way in in the past. Again, in the political world you kind of have your network, the network that is in power has some control over that. I don't think that in the past it had been so inviting to women. Which, as I said, I think even in my political experience—not too long [laughs]—it's changed drastically, so I think that's good. I think there are a lot [more] women running. I see there are more female candidates. I would add that particularly women of color have even more of a challenge with that than White women do in the city of Worcester. We don't see as many women of color in elected office, so I think there's still some lingering of that old mentality. I think it's come a long way, but obviously a ways to go.

I didn't get involved in politics until I was in college. My family was never really politically active, and I wasn't really before college. I think it's a lot of my belief system—which is interesting with 16 years of Catholic education—a lot of my belief system is just more [of a] progressive mentality. When we went into war, [while I was in college], I was very much against that. I've worked a lot for women in [what has been seen as] women's causes. I'm very pro-choice, pro-marriage equality, and things like that.

I actually already had a job lined up before I graduated. My sister was working as a shelter advocate at a shelter for battered women in Worcester. She used to run support groups with the women that were in the shelter and so the nights she did the support group, I ran a playgroup with the kids. Then during that experience and my time there, I got very much interested in that issue—I still do a lot of work around domestic violence. So around the time I was graduating, the children's advocate was leaving, so it worked out that they offered me that position. So I already had a job lined up.

My senior year in college I got involved in the gubernatorial race. I ended up my second semester senior year taking an internship in Congressmen [Jim] McGovern's office. So [I] worked really hard there. About a year working at the shelter, I ran into the congressman's chief of staff who was running for State Senate. It was the same election cycle for the congressman, so he offered me a position on the campaign. I worked on the campaign for the two of them, and then they both won. He went to Boston; he offered me a job in his office there. About four years later the mayor of Worcester, Tim Murray, decided to run for lieutenant governor. He became lieutenant governor, offered me a job because as I said, I had been very involved in his campaign, so got to know him in my time there. He was elected with Governor [Deval] Patrick, and then they offered me a position in the administration. So I worked in the governor's office for a year, and then went over to the lieutenant governor's office where I was for five years, five and a half years just about. Having those opportunities while I was in college, certainly opened up my opportunities post-grad. That was very helpful.

For the past six years I've been on the Board of Directors at the YWCA in Worcester which was very much at the time a hobby. And I was actually, for a few years, on the national YWCA board, which was an incredible experience. I got to go all over the country for meetings, and meet incredible women. YWCAs are doing different programming all over the place, so I get to learn what the folks are doing and all with the goal of serving women, and improving the lives of women and girls, and eliminating racism, which is our mission. That's kind of a big piece of who I am [laughs] and what I've been doing since graduating. That's really important because I worked there for a year and then even once I moved on, I still stayed engaged and went onto the board and it was an incredible experience.

There's a Governor's Council on Sexual and Domestic Violence that the lieutenant governor used to chair, and now the secretary of Health and Human Services chairs. [As deputy assistant secretary for Children, Youth and Families at the Massachusetts Executive Office of Health and Human Services], I've been the staff point person reaching out. I've gotten to work a lot on policy around domestic and sexual violence. I can certainly say government has taken a lot of strides to make not just services available—because again I think we can always do more—but to make the experience that women are going through easier for them and less of a burden. In fact there was legislation—I don't know if it just passed the House—but it just had some movement today in the legislature that would make some major changes to law to better protect and better serve women. Things from requiring that employers give women who are fleeing domestic violence time off to be able to address it without the risk of losing their job, so if they have to go to a court date, so that if they have to spend some time trying to find an apartment, a new apartment or spend some time at the doctors, whatever the case may be, that they don't have to risk losing their job to be able to do that. So I think government slowly but surely is getting there.

[Advice I would give to women?] I would say get involved and speak up. I think even as far as society has come, society still teaches us to take a back seat, to sit on the outsides of a meeting table. You'll see the men all come sit at the table and you'll often still see women sit around the outsides. So I would say sit at the table. It's still going to be very rare that somebody invites you in, so sometimes as uncomfortable as it may be, you have to invite yourself in. And then I would say something certainly that I have tried to do, is pay it forward. You're given an opportunity; pay it forward to someone behind you because we're our best allies and our best advocates, so it's our responsibility to bring other women along with us.

Louise Gleason
Age 67
Interviewed on November
13, 2006 by Jessica Roberts
and Marc Ebacher of
Assumption College
Overseen by Prof. Brian
Niece, Assumption College

I went to St. Vincent Hospital School of Nursing, which is no longer in existence. And then I went to Anna Maria College and I got a bachelor's later on when I was in my 40s, and got my master's when I was in my 50s, and, staying with education, now I'm in W.I.S.E. [Worcester Institute for Senior Education], and still going to school.

I was 17. It was an unbelievable experience. Back then our probationary period ended after six months. Many of the kids in my class [our ages were 16, 17, 18 years old], were put in charge of whole floors [called units now] at night, from 11 to 7. That would never happen now, you know. Can you see like a little 18-year-old having responsibility for very sick people? That's what was expected of you.

Will you believe this? Three hundred-fifty dollars for three years! That included everything. But see where they got a lot of work out of us? And they didn't pay us, of course. So, that was it, $350. I had $350 in the bank—I had $375 and that was it [laughs].

[I worked at] Worcester State Hospital. I did that for a long time and then I went to work at the Department of Mental Health. [It] had clinics in downtown Worcester for mental health, and that was an expanded role for nursing because nurses, up until that point, never did therapy. They just were situated in the hospital and they pass pills and that was it, you know, and managed floors. But now this was an expanded role for nursing where they would be doing psychotherapy with patients, group therapy, and psychopharmacology therapy with them, so we had a lot of patients to deal with, a lot. The nurses had more patients than the docs [doctors], and social workers, and psychologists because they were all with the state hospital patients. They were really the worst and the hardest ones to deal with, and so our caseloads would be 150. Not that you'd see them every day. And there'd always be a crisis because they were from that time where they were emptying out the state hospitals, and they hadn't provided appropriate treatment and places for them to live. So you were continuously doing not only therapy, but social work types of things for them, and trying to get them resituated when they'd get kicked out of their housing. It was—it was quite a challenge.

I loved that part of nursing. That is nursing. We did the expanded role and it—we were like pioneers in developing this new role for nursing, which continues to this day. So, when nurses didn't do therapy before, we certainly were the ones out there early on doing that, and allowing nurses to go forward with that.

[I worked as a nurse for] 39 years! [Laughs] I went back to Worcester State Hospital for a short time, and then I went to the University of Massachusetts and that's where I ended my career. I got a clinical specialist certification through the American Nurses Association, and my position was the in-patient unit and I pretty much—I did a lot of the day-to-day management and all—I oversaw the total care of all the patients there. I had great nurses that were there, but I had to keep an eye on not only the nurses, but the docs, social workers, and whoever else was there! [Laughs] Make sure everybody was on track.

But I loved my work. Absolutely. It was so hard, it was so intense at some times, and sometimes physically, physically dangerous, but I absolutely loved it. The part I loved—once I went out to the community, and got a taste of actually working in that one-to-one with patients, I really loved it. And it was a position [in which] you could grow professionally and personally. Even though it was hard and some days you just listened to the same problem over and over and over again, and you know it's not going to get any better. But for some reason, it really—I felt as though it did a lot for me, and maybe it was just that I could see that I was helping these people better than when I was in the hospital. And then I also loved my job at UMass too. That was really a wonderful job. But what happened, it just—there comes a time that you just say, "I don't want to do this anymore." And I did that one day.

When you're a nurse, you're everything. It isn't just that you do bedside nursing. It opens the door to so many different types of careers that I would recommend that to anybody that's interested in education or a career that's going to be helping. We did social work, we did,—now nurses can prescribe medication, they do therapy, they run clinics on their own, and they do all these high-level things that before they weren't able to do, but now with expanded roles and acceptance in higher education, they just, they're right up there.

Amy Szarkowski
Age 34
Interviewed on April 8, 2008 by Samantha Murphy of
College of the Holy Cross
ASL Interpreters: Caity Cross-Hansen and Catherine
Calender of Northeastern University
Overseen by Prof. Judy Freedman Fask, College of the
Holy Cross

My friend was 20 years old at the time, when her hearing started to decrease and she began learning ASL [American Sign Language]. She was adopted and raised by her adopted parents. When at 20 years old she went to the doctor and he told her that she would become deaf, well it scared the life out of her. The two of us decided to start taking ASL classes and I just fell in love with the language, with the community, I just loved it right from the beginning. So when I was 22 or 23, I decided that I wanted to work with Deaf people.

My roommate is also studying psychology, she herself is hard of hearing, but growing up she didn't use sign language. When she did start to learn it, she learned it quickly. The two of us started at Gallaudet [University, a world leader in education for deaf and hard of hearing students], but were both a bit nervous since we both were not good signers at the time. I had worked for years at Kentucky Prep School, so I thought that my signing was pretty good. But once I entered Gallaudet, I realized that there were much better signers than I was. When I entered, it was a little shaky at first but after I got a little bit better, the situation became easier. I went to college for five years, one year I spent abroad though in Italy, so really I only spent four years studying here at Gallaudet.

I've had two experiences working with Gallaudet. I was an advisor for two years to Deaf children, and then I was an advisor to other Deaf children and adults, and then my current job here at the hospital that I'm dealing with more medical situations now. Such as, children come in who have cancer, and the drugs they are taking to treat it have made them become deaf, so the reasons that I'm dealing with Deaf children here are different than they were before. I deal with more serious medical issues now.

I really enjoy working with children. One of my personal goals is to learn more about neurological psychology, I'm currently in training for that now, and it's been a wonderful experience. So to learn more about that is my personal goal. My professional goal is to help improve the program I am currently in. I hope to see more Deaf children. Currently there are two full-time psychologists working here, and I'm a trainee. I hope that by next year I will be a full-time psychologist here as well. So really my professional goal is to help this program improve its services for Deaf children.

I'm not yet an expert at sign language, I hope to be, but [I'm] not there yet. I want to continue learning and improving my signing skills. But compared to most psychologists in the Massachusetts area, other places as well, I know a lot about the Deaf community. When psychologists are dealing with deaf children and don't know anything about the Deaf community, it can be dangerous. It's possible that they could refer them to the wrong person, or give them the wrong recommendation. They may blame the deafness for their problems when really it's a totally separate issue.

I think parents have different levels of accepting their deaf children. When they start out, they're really defensive, and they may have their child's hearing tested many, many times. They just can't accept that their child is actually going deaf. Then they may begin to accept it more when they begin to learn sign language and when they meet other parents in the same situation as they are. So it really depends on the parents themselves and which level they're at in the process.

Many Deaf people are defensive about cochlear implants. But now the times have changed a bit. [Some culturally] Deaf people are still pretty defensive, but some, along with other younger deaf people, are realizing that the cochlear implants are occurring more often. They [are concerned] that the Deaf population will shrink. What they need to understand is that when a child has an implant, their hearing isn't perfect and they have to go through a lot of training. My personal concern is that children with implants often are mainstreamed in public school, and they are isolated there and don't have any connections to other students with cochlear implants. That can really be devastating to their self-esteem. The Deaf culture is wonderful at boosting a child's self-esteem; it gives them a sense of identity, which I think is important for all children. So my personal hope is that the Deaf culture continues to be strong, but at the same time [the community] makes sure that deaf children with cochlear implants aren't isolated, and that they do feel they have a place where they can connect with each other.

Matilde Castiel
Age 56
Interviewed in Spanish on March 23, 2011 by Marie Theroux, Kaitlyn Fagundes, Catherine Griffin of Assumption College Translated from Spanish to English by Ariana Babigian, Kerry Thomas, Caitlyn White, Andrew Trottier of Assumption College

Overseen by Profs. Maryanne Leone and Esteban Loustaunau, Assumption College

I was born in Cuba. I remained there until the age of seven years—six and a half to seven years and then I

came to the United States in a program called Peter Pan—
Operation Peter Pan. I stayed in a foster home [laughs]
for a few months until my parents came to California.

Operation [Peter Pan] happened—I came in '62,
but it started in '61. Thousands of young people left Cuba
and it was something that was done by the American
government and the American church that helped to bring
thousands of children here. I left when I was six, my
brother was eight years old and we came here and first
they sent us for a while, two weeks in Miami, and then we
went to Los Angeles, and we stayed there three months
until my parents came. And I didn't know English, but I
learned English in three months. When my parents came,
I still couldn't live with them because they didn't have a
job, and they didn't have money. The organization that
brought me here was the Jewish Family Services. Jewish
Family Services also helped my dad and my mom to find
jobs, but until they had jobs and had an apartment, I
couldn't live with them.

It was difficult to adjust to life in the United
States. I had to leave my parents in Cuba, and I came with
a woman that I did not know. I went to school without
knowing how to speak English. So, this was very difficult.
After, when my parents came, things became better for
me. However, it was more difficult for them because they
were now living in a new culture, a new language.

I moved to Worcester because of my husband.
My husband and I met in St. Louis, Missouri, and we were
doing our medical residency there, and he wanted to come
to Massachusetts to try something new. And I was just his
girlfriend then. So he decided to move and when he asked
me to marry him, he was already here. So I had to move
with him. So he told me that it would only be for two
years, and we now have been living here for 20 years.

I work for the University of Massachusetts
Medical School and Hospital. I am a doctor. So, I have an
MD (Doctor of Medicine degree). My work is in the

community. I have clinics in Worcester Housing and I have clinics in Centro Las Américas, and most recently we started a program called The Héctor Reyes House and it is a program for young men or Latinos—Latino men with drug problems. It is a residential program.

[My decision to become a doctor] was partly in order to help people who had no money or an education—to help them with their medical problems. In high school, I really liked science classes. When I was in high school I worked in a hospital where I saw a surgery, a heart surgery, and I liked it very much. And I decided to do that. [The most rewarding aspect of being a doctor is being able] to help people who need help, and to be something positive in their lives. It has meant a lot because I have been able to help in the lives of many people and not only with their health issues, but in many aspects of their lives.

My dad had a sixth grade education and he always used to sell clothes and household items. And when he came to the United States, he came without any money. At the beginning, he took paint off furniture. He did this for a few months until he was able to buy his car. Then he went and bought clothes, sheets, and towels—all kinds of things. And then he put all the items in his car, and went to where the Mexicans lived in California because he could speak Spanish. There are many Mexicans in California and he sold all the things he had. He did that all his life, selling everything from behind his car. I do the same today with medicine because I have all of my things in the back of my car, and I go from place to place working like my father.

CHAPTER THREE

FINDING HER OWN PATH

Some stories don't have a clear beginning, middle, and end. Life is about not knowing, having to change, taking the moment and making the best of it, without knowing what's going to happen next. Delicious ambiguity.

Gilda Radner, comedienne, actress

Anh Vu Sawyer
Age 60
Interviewed on March 28, 2013
by Estanislau Pina and Donald
Vo of Assumption College
Overseen by Prof. Carl R.
Keyes, Assumption College

I was born in Saigon, Vietnam. When I came to this country, I was in Fort Chaffee, Arkansas, in the refugee camp. I was 22. From there we were sponsored by a church called Christ's Church in Oak Grove in Chicago, Illinois. After some months in the

146

refugee camp, once we were sponsored, we flew directly from the refugee camp to Chicago. That was in early 19— you know it's a crazy thing. We have no sense of time because there's no calendar when you run, and you stayed in refugee camps, and moved from camp to camp.

I was in medical school [in Vietnam] in the '70s. In the '70s no woman should be thinking of having an American boyfriend because only "ladies of the night" would be caught on the street with an American G.I Joe. Here I was, dreaming of my boyfriend as an American and so I went to—fast-forward to 1975—I came to this country. I met this man in college, and he looked exactly like that guy in my dream! The crazy thing is he noticed me first, and so that's how we met.

America spoils me with freedom because, even when I was in Vietnam, I always hungered for freedom. So when I met Phillip, when I first came here, I realized my goodness this is worth dying for. You see America gave me the freedom to be who I am, and also gave me the resources so that I can get what I want. Also, American people gave me an amazing example of giving themselves to others. I came from a culture where life was *so*, *so* hard.

For example when I was little, when we went to sleep, explosions could be all around us at night because that's the best time for the Vietcong to shell us. And so you'll never know when you'll get up and be alive or not. I slept with my little sister. She would be so scared and she pinched me. She dug her fingernails in my flesh every time we heard these huge explosions. So I told her, "Don't worry. We're going to die tomorrow. Tomorrow, we're going to be in heaven with God." Sometimes it would help her to go to sleep, but sometimes it didn't help me to go to sleep. So I daydreamed. One image always came to my mind. The American missionaries would give us their old Christmas cards, and I got this one of a photograph of a really small pretty Cape Cod-type house and there was snow outside, snow on the roof, snow on the driveway.

The sky was clear with the stars and there was a Christmas tree with all of these amazing colorful lights and small boxes with colors. I have always thought of it, that this must be heaven and I always wanted to be there. See where I am [now]?

We have three children. Two boys and one girl. They are the pride and the joy of our lives. They truly are. Especially when they sleep. If we both stayed in New York City, both of us would have to work. I quit my job so I could stay [home], and take care of our oldest boy. And so we decide to move to guess where? Kansas! To Lawrence, Kansas, and we had two more babies. [We spent] five years in Kansas. We really miss traveling. Right after I got married, I helped start an airline called People Express Airline. It's a very innovative company. I worked there for 10 years, but we travelled so much that when I stayed home to have our babies, we really missed [that]. We moved to Colorado [to work for a humanitarian organization] and we [were] in Colorado for 10, 15 years. Our heart is really close to humanitarian work.

I was in Vietnam last November and we [were] on our way to do our humanitarian work in the northern highlands. My husband and I help teach the Hmong women, who were victims of sex trafficking crimes, to sew. My husband also teaches at the Rhode Island School of Design. He taught sewing. So, we were on our way there and I got the email saying that this position was open. [And I thought] I would like very much to branch out and do something that I believe in and I'm good at. I saw this position [as executive director of the Southeast Asian Coalition of Central Massachusetts] open up. I looked at my email and I said that I would like to consider it.

When we meet immigrants here, they have such a hard time because of their English barrier and the culture is really difficult for them. And they have to work two jobs to help the family here, and help the family back home. When they came in I would interview them, and I found out that many of them have an amazing gift. Their gift is they know how to use their hands to make things. Something about Vietnamese—especially Southeast Asian—women. I'm starting the sewing program and then I found out from the Worcester Historical Museum that Worcester used to be the center of the industrial movement. This is my craziest dream, ridiculously crazy dream that my tiny little organization, we're going to start the industrial revival movement in Worcester with the sewing industry because we have the people who already have the skills.

I think in Vietnam the school system is much harder, very hard. I was in medical school, but our country could not afford to buy us textbooks. There was one textbook, one set for the whole entire school, so we had to do a lot of copying by hand. And because it's a medical school, the textbooks were in English. We had to decipher the English and the books were loaned to us, so they were the 20-years-old version. It's not current, but it's still wonderful. I appreciate the American way of education better. [In Vietnam] the students couldn't really ask a lot of questions. If we asked questions, we were considered as challenging the teacher. And I got into trouble all of the time. Can you imagine? I just asked a lot of questions. And the American system allowed us to have more room to think, to imagine. In Vietnam, they are interested in how much they can teach you and how much can you remember word by word.

I am very aware of politics. And I vote and I tell everyone they should vote, and I am liberal and visible enough out there for people to know what I would like because I'm very strong on social change and justice. [In Vietnam] it was the opposite. When I was in high school, I was so unhappy when I saw something that was not right. This was in South Vietnam now. I wrote an article. I was a writer ever since I was little and it was sent to the youth newspaper. And my mom found the article I was writing, and she tore it to shreds and she burned it. She said that if the authorities knew it, I'm in trouble. I was criticizing the authorities.

I feel like I'm a "daughter of the world" because I travel a lot and so I embrace my Vietnamese ethnicity very greatly. I learned so much from them, but I never felt that it is the only identity I have. I embrace my American influence and so when people ask me who I am, I always say I am Vietnamese by birth, but American by life.

Urszula Wierbik
Age 60
Interviewed on October 22, 2010 by Haley Andrews and Jamie Young of Assumption College
Overseen by Profs. Carl Keyes and Maryanne Leone, Assumption College

[My name is] Urszula Sprengel Wierbik. [I was born] in Poland. [My husband and I have] two children, girl and boy. I have three grandchildren.

My parents, they lived in north of Poland in the city called Slupsk and they were just typical Polish family. And in Poland, at the time we didn't have single houses. Most of the time in Europe in the complex apartments, there was usually four floors, sometimes three floors, and each floor was like a three family. That apartment was very small. We even didn't have the bathroom upstairs. We have to go downstairs on the first floor, and we live on the second floor. There was three bathrooms in the building. And each one belonged to that floor. So…it was horrible [laughing].

I came [to the United States] for medical reasons. And I came hoping to get help and I received the help. I came with my daughter. She was 10, and I had to leave my son over there with my husband. I was only covered [for] permission to come here with my daughter. [My husband came] later.

I am in a cleaning service business. First I was cleaning myself, and then I opened a service. I have the service now about 20 years. But I opened the service because I had so many customers. And I just realized I saved money better than nursing home, than nurse's aide, and there was flexible hours, there was mother's hours. And I had the children, so it was easy for me to do this kind of job. But I got so many clients I don't know what to do with them! So I opened a cleaning service.

I run the service with my daughter now. She graduate from college and she got married, she had child, so it is a great job for her because she's my partner. My son's helping me. He also is a college graduate. He has own business, but he helps me Friday. I'm getting old [laughs], so I need a Friday for myself and for my family.

[I've lived in Worcester] since 1982. Worcester is beautiful city, I like it, I enjoy [it] here. And I met some very interesting people through my job. I tried different jobs. I worked for the Digital Company in Marlboro. I worked as a nurse's aide, but for nursing homes. I wasn't very happy. I'm not the person to sit in assigned same place. And I consider that cleaning service business is very interesting. You meet a lot of people. You see how people live. Right now we are cleaning the Massachusetts College of Pharmacy for 10 years.

I'm vice president of the Worcester Polish Heritage Foundation in Worcester. Right now we have an exhibition in the Worcester Public Library. We have exhibition about Chopin and an exhibit about Katyn, a horrible place where Russian kills over 20,000 Polish officers, they murdered.

[I learned English] from my children. I took a few free classes, and just learned. Too bad I had no chance to go to the school because I was by myself with my daughter first, for a few years, then my son came, and my husband

151

came the last, so…I had to provide [laughs] bread for the table. And I build the house before my husband came.

I never thought I would stay here [in America]. It just happened. I am from a Communist country. We are not allowed to go anywhere, so you have no comparison. You cannot talk with other people. You are not allowed to go to other capitalist countries. If you don't know, you don't miss stuff. [A hard transition] for me [was] the language. First immigrants face always the worst [laughs]. It's easy for my children. They have the houses, they [are] educated, they think differently. That was my goal and it was solved.

I think we have a quite simple life, our pleasure is to travel. United States is beautiful. There is just so much to see. We just got back from Alaska. We worked hard saving money and go to the trip. But it was a big celebration; it was my 60th birthday party over there, and 40 years of marriage.

Well, I'm just ordinary person. It's just you have the duty to do and you just have to accomplish. I'm ordinary person, what's interesting with my story? Perhaps everybody have something to contribute.

Laurel Sanderson
Age 75
Interviewed on October 23, 2006 by Kristin Pancotti and Carolyn Kriso of Clark University
Overseen by Prof. Deborah Martin, Clark University

We lived in North Dakota. My first job, when my hands were strong enough, was learning to milk the cows. And hoeing in the garden. When we moved, I became a waitress, then the telephone company, and then I sold insurance for a little while. Then I went to work as a checker in the chain grocery store. Then I went to work in the bank, I was a jack-of-all-trades. I did accounts, kept track of the bad checks. And then I got married and came out here.

So part of your question was how did my early life, working on the farm, what I did on the farm, how did that affect my life? I think, really [pause] the greatest thing that could have happened. Because in essence what happened was that I have lived several different lives. One of them is my farm life, in North Dakota. And I wouldn't trade that for anything. Being able to grow up in the wide-open space, it does something for you. Everyone was poor, but nobody knew it because everybody was the same, because that was just the way it was.

My sister and I ended up doing things on the farm that some of the boys would have done, if they were older. She and I milked, and we did the separating. And we were responsible for keeping the pigs and the chickens fed. And you were down in that garden pulling like crazy all summer long, picking all the vegetables and everything, and helping [my mother] can.

Moving to South Dakota was not my idea. I waitressed, went to high school, graduated, met the man who would become my husband when I was just 16. I met him on my 16th birthday. We established our roots, and started raising kids. We were smart enough to stop at two. The marriage was getting very shaky. Eventually I had to go to work. I tried selling insurance and I'm not good at that, so I went to work at the grocery store as the checker.

But we were divorced. Eventually I went to work for the bank. It was during that time that I met the man from here that I married. He came into town, and then we left. Sounds simple. I came back here to live. I left behind my kids, my home, my mother (because my father was already dead), my siblings, my job, my friends, my church. Absolutely everything that meant anything to me, I left behind. Came out here, married to a man that I had known for six months.

I have discovered over time, that when it comes to large decisions like that, I just kind of put one foot in front of the other, and it isn't until years later that I realize that that was the best thing I could have done. It's like I'm inner-directed somehow. It just sort of moves me. He urged me to go to college. So I started over at Quinsig [Quinsigamond Community College]. I started out with one course per semester. I thought it was pretty good. He told me that I had too good a mind to waste without getting more of an education. Coming out here was one of the better things that I could have done. Because I was able to grow tremendously here, not only go to school, but I learned so many other things. My son never came out here, and he finished high school and he went in the Navy. My daughter came out here, and she went to the Navy— they both got off to good starts. And I think it was very helpful to them to see their mother be brave. And take big steps. Scary steps. And my granddaughter tells me the same thing. She said, "Grandma, if you can live by yourself, then I can live by myself." And so she does, in Chicago. And those things wouldn't have happened had I stayed there and muddled along. So, it's been good.

Well I'll tell you, there are some times when you better grow, or you're dead. The man I was married to could be a really marvelous person, he could be really intellectual. I sharpened my mind on his all of the time. But he's manipulative, and controlling. You either learn or you suffer the consequence. So, with John I learned a new language. Listened to him talk. What words did he use or not use? What tone of voice did he use? What was his expression? What was his body language? I learned all of those things. Stands me in good stead ever since because now I see people in a different way. I learned how to integrate with people who I always thought were way beyond me, socially speaking. I was just a farm girl, and we didn't know about etiquette. I learned how to travel; I learned how to go to school. I earned my associate degree from Quinsigamond, and I earned my Bachelor of Science in Business Administration from Clark [University] and my Master's in Business Administration from Clark. For me, education was a gift to myself.

If I look at my experience with State Mutual, because that's the one place that I've worked here, and it's been about 40 years since I started working there, women were not treated all that well. They didn't get paid what men were being paid. I had friends who were top supervisors in departments who had managers who would leave, and you would think that these people would move into that position because they've been there for a long time and they knew all the work down flat, but they always hired someone else that she'd have to train. So there was a time essentially when I came, where if you fell in love with a guy from the company, and you got married, one of you had to leave. And guess who that would be?

It was just assumed [on the farm] that everybody worked. The only reason you didn't work is if you were too ill to do so, or if you didn't have enough knowledge, and even then, those kids still had their chores to do too. All of my life, work was just something that you did. There's a joy in doing a job and doing it well; and having challenges thrown at you and being able to respond to them—and do a damn good job at it.

The benefits, I think, for myself, were, or are, a great deal of self-confidence. If I can get through Clark for crying out loud, if I can get through an MBA over there I can do goddamned anything! *Get your education.* That, to me, is the most important thing. After that, think about getting married. Because you might still get married for the wrong reason, you're trying to get away from home, you know you have some physiological needs or something, but at least you don't have to marry somebody because you've got to have someone support you. Why do you think I tell you that I got all that education I had? I was divorced by the time that I started my master's degree, but I divorced twice anyhow. And I finally came to the conclusion that there was nobody out there who was going to take care of me. Try to do things that build your self-esteem, and education can do that, so that you have strength as an individual, so that you don't have to lean on somebody else. Do the hard work because you want to learn. And the more you learn, the better you are.

Isabel González-Webster
Age 32
Interviewed in Spanish on April 1, 2011 by Ashley Swartz, Brendan Covey, and Marian Murphy of Assumption College
Translated form Spanish to English by Kim Parretti, Alex Caulway, and Melissa McLain of Assumption College
Overseen by Profs. Maryanne Leone and Esteban Loustaunau, Assumption College

I was born in Brooklyn, New York. My experience [there] was good. There were many Latinos. I grew up surrounded by Latino people and many people of color. So, I felt very comfortable. I think many people study for their career at the university. I learned in the street, in organizations. After I graduated from high school, I had two jobs. One teaching about how to make documentaries, and the second as an organizer about issues related to the environment, about asthma, about poor communities, and things like that. I learned from different people with whom I worked and that is how I learned what I need today.

When I lived in New York, when I began my career, one of my jobs was working with Latino immigrants who received social service support. And the campaign I worked for was about providing translation services in welfare centers. We had to organize, provide training, and frankly, sue the city [laughs]. Under civil rights law, anyone has access to public services no matter your race or language. If you have people in need of services, but who do not speak English—in welfare centers—and you do not provide them with translation services, you are keeping them away from public aid. So, now I have worked with a lot with Latinos. I also worked for an organization for young women of color: African-Americans, Latinas. So, I also did a lot of work on women's rights and against domestic violence.

I lived in New York since I was born until 2004. I had a car accident and I decided to take some time off. Then I moved with my partner to Puerto Rico, to the mountains of Mayagüez. I spent a year and a half there. I was offered a job in California, in Massachusetts, and in Maryland and I decided on Massachusetts. So, I have been here since November of 2005. I moved from the paradise that is Puerto Rico to Massachusetts.

I work in the mayor's office [as chief of staff]. [My daily routine] varies [laughs]. I arrive here and I check a lot of emails, return calls. We have many projects here. The mayor has a Commission for Latino Education in the city of Worcester. The commission is looking at how we can [improve] the education of Latino students here because, I believe, 36% of students in the Worcester public schools are Latinos. We were at this meeting where people were discussing what we can do to improve education in the schools and what are some recommendations.

Today my day started by checking lots of emails. I prepared for a meeting about looking for ways to find revenue for the city, for the state, to create jobs and services. Some of my responsibilities for today were to make sure that Monday's meeting will go well. I also went from that meeting to the one with the Latino Commission. [The mayor] has many goals and wants to achieve them. So, we do lots of projects. We could be working on small businesses, or on schools, or on taxes, on all kinds of things [laughs]. I'm never bored.

I never, never thought that I would work for the government. I thought that I would always work on the street with the community, doing organized work here in Worcester. I saw a need to bring the community and the government closer together, to open lines of communication, and to assure that the people in the community know that the government is here for them. And also that the government knows that it has to respond to the community. The biggest thing that I've learned is that in this city, one has to be involved in local government. If not, your voice is not heard.

I think that as a Latina woman, a person of color, I see that there is a difference in the way that I am treated. The services provided to me, and my community, and my family [should be the same] provided to White people, to people with more money. So, since the beginning I saw the difference. But instead of saying, "Well, that's the way things are," I've always had the energy to want to change things. I've always wanted justice. And I will die wanting social justice.

Kilbyanne Garabedian
Age 65
Interviewed on October 29, 2010
by Bethany Bartalani and
Kimberly Leighton of
Assumption College
Overseen by Profs. Carl Keyes
and Maryanne Leone, Assumption
College

In my high school yearbook, you know how you have your picture and then they have all these little sayings underneath? One of the sayings under my name was that I wanted to be the first female cardiac surgeon in the United States, because there weren't any female cardiac surgeons at that time. I really wanted to be a physician, but the support wasn't there. Now I have to admit there were women and girls who did become physicians. So if I had more motivation and a really burning desire, I think I could have done it, but there certainly wasn't the support.

I went to a nursing school—a diploma school for nursing. And then I went to Assumption College and graduated with a BS [Bachelor of Science]. I actually did pre-med there. Assumption College at that time had a very good acceptance rate into medical school. I was married and had kids by that time, so I couldn't go to school in the traditional manner and so actually the Continuing Education Department designed my curriculum so that I could do pre-med. What they allowed me to do was take a certain number of courses through Continuing Ed., and then the same amount of courses through the day program. It was a little bit of a challenge because I was an older person. I remember an exam that we had, and I'd been sick and I was taking Sudafed, but I decided, "I can I can handle this." And then, of course, my kids got sick. I was up all night with them, and then my husband got sick. And I was sitting next to a young woman who played tennis, and she was all upset because she was having a meet with somebody, and she had never seen her opponent serve before. And I just kind of looked at her and I thought, "We are from different universes here." [Laughs]

One of my professors said to me that I wrote very descriptively and asked, "Have you ever thought about going to law school?" Now, ironically, at the same time in my nursing career, there were some things happening in the law. Karen Ann Quinlan and Nancy Cruzan were two young women who were very badly injured. They were in vegetative states. I was very interested in that because I was in critical care and we were resuscitating people who

159

had a right to die. They were at the end of life, and we were imposing treatment. So I was very interested in that, so those two things kind of worked together and I thought maybe I'll look into this, see what this law is all about. And I [took] a couple of classes and I really enjoyed it. So I decided to go to law school. So I took the LSAT's [Law School Admission Test], did well, and here I am.

When I got to law school, it was the same type of thing because I had to work. I went to Suffolk [University]. You could go nights. In order to get experience, you had to go to the volunteer defender's or the volunteer prosecutor's office and that was a day thing. I couldn't do that, I was working full time. So I kind of figured out a way to get in touch with [the] general counsel at Memorial Hospital and we created an internship program for me. So I guess the point you asked, "If there were any challenges?" the challenges at that time were that education was not set up for adults and part-time students. I think today it is much more flexible and people can go part time, they can work full time. You can do a lot of different kinds of things that weren't acceptable then.

I worked with two small law firms. One is no longer in existence and that was in Grafton, the other one was in Holden. I went to law school to become a hospital lawyer. When I started working with the one in Holden, one of the senior partners is on the board here at this hospital, UMass [University of Massachusetts] Memorial. And I'd had a relationship, as I said, with the general counsel because he and I created this internship program when I was in school. As a position opened, they asked me if I would like it. And I said I absolutely would and I've been here ever since.

What has [my job as associate general counsel for UMass Memorial Health Care] meant to me? Well, I really like my job. One of the things, unfortunately, is sometimes as a nurse, at least years ago, you didn't have the credibility in patient care. Becoming a lawyer gave me that credibility. I can help patients by helping their care providers, by providing a legal framework for physicians and nurses, so that they can feel comfortable taking care of the patients. In terms of the law and in terms of being worried about being sued, they can focus on those patients and take excellent care of those patients, and I feel very rewarded about that. And somebody else must, too, because I got an award this year from *Lawyers Weekly* about that, so somebody agrees with my analysis.

I like the path I chose. I've had a wonderful opportunity to have about four careers. I teach at the medical school so I've been a nurse, a lawyer, a teacher, a mother—all of those. They're all wonderful opportunities and I'm very happy that I've been able to do that. I think if you'd ask my children, they would say that when I went to law school, they felt disconnected with me. Because now [that] we're all adults, we sit around and talk about that sometimes. And it was hard at the time from my side to continue doing what I wanted to do with them. They were all very involved in sports at the time, playing football, playing field hockey; I wanted to go to all of their games. That was all challenging. I don't think that I would have done anything differently. I've told my husband the only thing I would do differently, is I would have married him sooner, but I was only 20 when I got married.

Barbara Kohin
Age 80
Interviewed on March 20, 2013
by Thomas Ashe, Chelsea
Gamboa, and Kaitlyn Murphy of
Assumption College
Overseen by Prof. Carl Keyes,
Assumption College

My father was a biologist. And my mother also studied biology, although she didn't work in the field. My father was a biology professor. My family had a sort of scientific tendency gene. One of my sisters is an engineer, a civil engineer, and the other one had a PhD in chemistry, and I'm a physicist. And, in my father's family, there were quite a few scientists also.

I went to graduate school in Maryland which is where I met my husband. We were both studying physics. And after that we went to Geneva, Switzerland, for a short time. Then Roger got a job at Clark [University], and so we came directly to Clark, to Massachusetts in the '60s, early '60s. And we've been here ever since.

I went to [the College of] William and Mary as an undergraduate, and I majored in chemistry. I graduated in 1953 and I went to [University of] Maryland. I was sort of recruited by Maryland. They were building a Physics Department. They came into our school and recruited some of us chemists to do chemical physics. I had applied for a job in my senior year. I had a friend who worked for GE [General Electric] and I went up to Schenectady for an interview because I saw this program. It was a program that offered training in nuclear power, and I thought that sounded great. They had this kind of a fellowship or trainingship, so I went to GE. Well, this is like the dark ages and I sort of pushed myself in for an interview to the department but he said, "We don't take women in that program at all." I was a little taken aback. But that is how it was back in those days. "They just get married. We just spend all this money on training and they just get married." And he was just awful. And I said, "Well I'm serious!" Because I was a serious student. And he said, "Oh just come back when you get your PhD." I always thought to myself that I would go back because when I got my PhD, physicists were very much in demand. I would get the interview, and they would offer me the job, and I would say, "I wouldn't take your job if it was the last thing in the world." But it seemed like a lot of trouble just for revenge, so I didn't do it [laughs].

Well those were the days. It was very different for women. They had help wanted [ads] for women and help wanted for men. I was the only woman in physics at that time. I mean it seemed that there were so few of us. Of course, now there are lots and lots. My sisters and I were just sort of brought up to not think about sexual stereotypes. We didn't conform to the usual.

When I first came to Worcester, the colleges didn't hire women. I sent my resume to WPI [Worcester Polytechnic Institute], [College of the] Holy Cross, Assumption [College]. I sent my resumes around, and they didn't even answer. They didn't respond or acknowledge. I remember I thought I'd call up WPI and talk to the physics guy and he said, "Well, we do have an opening for a molecular physicist" and I said, "I am a molecular physicist!" [Laughs] And he said, "Really?" I never got an interview. So I did get a job finally at Worcester State [University]. I had a really terrible load and I had four courses and two labs. I got myself elected to the state college [association]. We observed the trustees' meetings and so I started having my own meetings at Worcester State. The president didn't really enjoy this too much. It was sort of riling up the faculty a bit. I only stayed three years. I quit actually. Every time my husband had a sabbatical, I quit my job. So, I had a series of different jobs. But I quit the job at Worcester State because there was a job at Clark [University] for a year filling in for someone.

Then we went to Yugoslavia for sabbatical. Yugoslavia, then we had India. We also spent a year in Africa in Kenya. It was such a good experience. And we spent a year in Geneva. And back then I went to Holland for a bit.

I was on several different boards a few years ago, and I've retired from those. Now all I have is the

[Worcester Women's] History Project and I think I am going to go off that board next fall. My term is up. I must have been on 35 boards and community organizations. I joined a lot of stuff. Maybe because I was interested in politics, or because people knew I was in politics and they asked me to join things. I was head of the ACLU [American Civil Liberties Union] Chapter and founded this Soviet Sister Project when I was at Holy Cross—sort of a peacenik kind of thing. I was trustee at the public library. I was the chairman of the trustees at the public library. So I have been in a lot.

[What have women in Worcester's experiences been like?] Well, they certainly have progressed politically. I mean we now have, what three women on the City Council, I think? [I was one of the first three women elected to the Worcester City Council.] We had three women in '73 and that was out of nine. We've never had one-third of the council as women since that period. It was rather a fluke; our election was quite a fluke. I mean we all lost in two years. We snuck up on them [laughs].

I think we have a much more professional City Council than we did when I was in office. It was like a family business then. It was not a well-run city, in many respects. But it is now. Much better. I think there are more women active in politics. We have a woman [state] senator, and we have a woman [state] representative now, Mary Keefe. And I don't remember ever having—we never had another legislator. Although we had the first woman senator, she's been there for a long time. We had the first woman representative from Worcester, I mean this is incredible.

Patricia Jones
Interviewed on October 17,
2013 by Nicholas Curello and
Priscilla Rodriguez of
Assumption College
Overseen by Profs. Leslie
Choquette and Allison Meyer,
Assumption College

My father was older
when he married my mother, which was common for the
quote old Irish families. I believe he was 48 when he
married my mother. He had spent lots of years in the
[United States] Navy. And when he settled back in
Worcester, he was a firefighter. My mother had moved to
the Worcester area and was one of 12, and during the
Depression the families relocated to where there were
jobs. There were lots of mill jobs in the Worcester area, so
she relocated to Worcester and met my father. They
married, and my sister and I were born. [I grew up near]
Chandler Street/Jaques Ave. It was very poor, and it was a
difficult environment to live in.

As a child, I attended parochial schools here in
Worcester and some of this is probably reflective of this
neighborhood that I was brought up in. I quit school
when I was 16, and in this neighborhood, that was not an
uncommon occurrence. It was more common than not,
and it was at 16, or shortly thereafter, that I married for
the first time. And [it wasn't] until after I had more
children that I decided that I was going to need an
education, and started first to get my GED [General
Equivalency Diploma], which was an easy
accomplishment, and then Quinsig [Quinsigamond
Community College] part-time evenings to start to work at
obtaining an education. I think that Quinsigamond
Community College has made a major contribution to
allow a huge population to obtain education that wouldn't

be available to them. Right about that time, I was divorced and needed to get a job. I continued going to school part time at night and obtained my bachelor's degree. At the time there was not even [an accounting] degree available in Worcester County. It was necessary for me to commute to Boston. I actually landed my first full-time and decent paying job at a bank that was a high promoter of education, and I obtained my graduate degree while working at the bank.

By the time I was going to graduate school, I had determined that accounting, and what's associated with taxes, was where my career was. I had done some work in public accounting before I went to the bank, and found the bank a tremendous opportunity. But it was more narrow, and I decided to go back to public accounting. I have been effectively on my own now for 30 plus years, so I haven't worked for anyone else for 30 something years.

I would suspect that my destiny was to be on my own and not to have a boss. I enjoy what I do. I like accounting. I like taxes. I like public accounting. I wish that there were more women. Particularly for younger women that are here and gaining their experience, I tell them that my job is to encourage them to stay in public accounting. The accounting part of the work, I don't consider it a job. Even as I told you about the 60-hour schedule, I do that for choice. No one says I have to, and I don't have a schedule that I need to meet or keep. I don't watch TV, and it's what I do.

In hindsight do I have regrets? I would not encourage anyone to quit school. I would not encourage anyone to get married when they're 17. I would [laughs] probably not encourage people to do a lot of things that I did. However, an individual is a composite, and if I didn't have some of those experiences, would I be the same?

Mary Melville
Interviewed on October 19, 2006 by Carolyn Kriso and
Kristin Pancotti of Clark University
Overseen by Prof. Deborah Martin, Clark University

I was born in Cairo, Egypt. My father was British
and my mother was Italian. In my generation, in England,
less than two percent of women went to college, and I
wanted to go to college. I said to my father, "I want to go
to England to pursue my studies." And he said, "Well, I
don't have enough money for you to go to England,
because what money I've got, I've got to save for your
brother, because he's got to have an education and raise a
family." It was one of my first realizations that I wasn't a
boy. He said, "I'll tell you what. You work for a year, and
I'll double that amount and you can go to college for
however long that lasts." So I worked at three jobs and
almost broke his bank [laughs].

I went to England and went to the Polytechnic
Institute, where I found myself up against scientists, and
my interest was more natural science. And then my
brother died, so I had to ship back to Egypt for what I
thought was going to be a short time. But my parents
were so devastated that I spent three years there. I went to
night school. I studied economics and statistics.

I looked for a job in London, and was very
fortunate. In the '50s in England there were plenty of job
opportunities, and I just applied to several openings. I had
an interview with a head of an economics department in
the Dunlop Rubber Company, which was then a very big
international company. And I had an interview with this
guy, and we had this long talk on what we were both
interested in—music. So we talked about music and he
eventually hired me [laughs]. So my life has been a series
of happenstances. It's not unusual in a lot of very
successful adults. It's kind of who you go up in the

elevator with, who you happen to meet, that changes the direction of your life

Three years later, I had gone from doing statistical research to doing reports for the board of directors, which was relatively prestigious, and doing some forecasts for materials that they bought, like rubber for cars. I went to the chief of the whole department, and I said, "Why don't you promote me the way you promoted the other two men?" And he said, "You realize that you are one of the three most senior women in the company." I said, "That's all very well, but the other two women are secretaries." [Laughs] That was the attitude.

I didn't [get the promotion] because, as he said, I was a turncoat. I left to get married and left town [laughs.] So I proved him right. You can't trust women. They get married! I went to Harvard [University], actually. I got a job as a statistician in the Department of Economics. Harvard Business School did not have women there, and the atmosphere in the '50s was, we were supposed to be good wives. We were supposed to cook breakfast, and, I'm quoting, send our husbands off to their important work. We were supposed to not bother them with the minutiae of family life, and then they'd come home, and we'd have dinner ready, and we'd do whatever we had to do to be good social adjuncts.

They all had degrees from prestigious women's colleges, but none of those [women] were aspiring to be anything but good wives. The general kind of atmosphere, certainly in places like Harvard Business School, was to me, appalling. I went home and cried. I said, "I don't want to hear this stuff." They'd call me and say, "We're having a wives' tea. Would you make some cookies?" I'd never made cookies in my life! And I still don't! [Laughs] But anyway, they didn't throw me out. My husband grew up with five very strong women so he grew up with a respect for the other sex.

We went to New York because he got a job. [I was] 27. I'd had three years' experience in London as a statistical research associate. I had two years working as a statistician in the Department of Economics under [John Kenneth] Galbraith [laughs]. I had experience as well as a strange background in education. I went to interview for a job. I thought TWA would be good because we really liked to travel. And I was turned down by the two men who were the personnel [managers and who] said, "We have the openings, you fit the bill, you have the experience, but I can't replace a man by a woman." It was kind of accepted! They didn't even have to hide [it]!

I went [to Time Inc.] and had the best interview I've ever had in my life. And so, the woman who was head of personnel said, "You've got a wild résumé, lived in all kinds of places, speak languages. You're just the crazy kind of person that we like. So I look at *Fortune* and, she said, "If you come to work for *Fortune*, you will be a researcher. The men are the writers, the women are the researchers, and you will never get a byline. I said, "OK!" It was better than not having a job. So that was the time when we broke through. And it was also about that time that people like Gloria Steinem and others were making a lot of noises. And what we were all fighting for was availability of jobs and equal pay. What we didn't fight for, and this is in retrospect, was choice. Not choice in terms of pro or against abortion, but choice that if I decide that I want to use my time raising a family, that's alright too. Because if I hire you as a governess, or I hire you to wash my floors, you have a job. But if I do it in my own home, I don't have a job. And so, you were kind of looked down on, in my group, if you didn't have a job and you weren't a professional.

I also worked here at Clark [University] as part of a research group, which is now the Marsh Institute, and that was happenstance too. After my husband retired, I realized that if I were to pursue my work opportunities, I was going to have to go back to school. I would have to spend a lot more time, and go to conferences, and everything else. I chose not to. And I had to decide that the accolade and my self-respect were not dependent on my worth in money, and that was very difficult, because we tend to judge our worth in dollars. I was never going to make the money that Don has made, and I was never going to give the time, so that I could spend time with my children and then later with my grandchildren. I was never going to be CEO [Chief Executive Officer] of a company, and in my generation, there weren't many. There are now, but not many.

I was invited on boards and when the subject was right, or the need was right, I became chair of the board. I was chair of the board of Mechanics Hall and I was chair of the board at the EcoTarium, which is the local natural science museum. So I guess one of the things that moves me is that I want to be useful to society, I want to earn my place in the sun. And I can be useful without being paid. And that came hard, but I understood it. And it's something that I learned in Worcester, because it's not the tradition in Europe.

I was able to make that choice, because I was not financially dependent on my job and I don't know how I would have felt if I'd had to work to put food on the table constantly. So if I had to juggle a lot, I was very fortunate in that I could control the amount of juggling I did.

Lisa Raymon
Age 46
Interviewed on March 16, 2012
by William Rein and Brian
Hulley of Assumption College
Overseen by Prof. Carl Keyes,
Assumption College

I graduated valedictorian of my high school. I really wasn't sure, I had a few things going on so, I attended Suffolk University for a few semesters, and then left there. I eventually went to Northeastern [University's] nursing school. I never finished, then I became a mother. When I moved out to this area back in 2003, I attended Rob Roy Academy in Worcester for cosmetology and graduated from there in 2004. I opened my hair salon on West Boylston Street.

I loved school. If I could go back to school to be a professional student, I would love that [laughs]. We had a lot of issues growing up. My dad was an alcoholic, and we had a lot of family issues in reference to that. When I was 16, I was date raped—that was part of the reason I faltered in college—and did not tell anybody for 20 years. I was the brain. I worked, I did basketball. So, when it happened to me, it was big. I couldn't tell anybody because, "I am too smart for that," not trying to bother anybody. It quite honestly affected my life for a good first half of it, at least.

If you were to ask me this question 20 years ago I probably wouldn't have told you, but that was the big thing for me in gaining my own footing again confidence-wise. I was supposed to go to Boston College, and I was supposed to do all this stuff, but when your head isn't right, you do a lot of transition things. I never had any problems with academics or working. It was all the emotional stuff that I dealt with in reference to that. I did eventually tell my family, as an obligation, so it wouldn't happen to them, and if it did, then it's OK to talk about, no matter what. For my children, my son has a lot of respect for women, and my daughters are very, very strong and they each have a boyfriend. They have also learned from my experience. They needed to know.

I had a lot of support, but when you live a life in secret, which I ended up doing, that part does not come into play because you can't really talk to anybody about it.

171

My parents were very wonderfully loving people. The whole reason [I didn't tell them] was I did not want to disappoint them.

I started working when I was 11. I babysat and then I got a job with the newspaper distribution office. When my children were younger, I did other jobs. I worked for a student loan company. I did records management, customer service, collections. I waitressed. I started my own cleaning company which allowed me to set my own hours. When my kids didn't need me as much, I went back to school. I worked when their father was home, so one of us was always with the children.

When I met my husband, establishing a life together, having children, mostly taking care of them and doing all of that [was very important]. We had a lot of hard financial times. Then [after] the dissolution of the marriage, which was something that I wanted, I went back to school to become a cosmetologist. I wanted more from life than just work, kids, and a marriage that wasn't working. Now, I can set my own schedule, but I basically do work Tuesday through Saturday. One thing I would like to do is to go back to school and do something, as it was always a goal to finish my education. [I was] very sidetracked, which is why I tell my kids, "Don't get sidetracked" [laughs]. So, all the stuff I have been through has put me to the point where I can run a business. I've been doing it for five years and I'm still able to do it. So, I take my success from that, that I am doing OK.

As a child I was always kind of sickly. They never knew why and all these weird things were wrong with me. My breastbone stuck out, my feet were flat, I was always having rashes. When I was pregnant with my son, my sister read an article about a condition called Marfan Syndrome, which is a connective tissue disorder. She said, "Well that sounds like Lisa." So in little bold print [it said]: "People with full blown Marfan Syndrome should be careful when they give birth." Apparently, your aorta could burst. Well I was in with the cardiologist seven and one half months pregnant and yes I do have it. And basically, any part of your body that has connective tissue is affected, it just depends on how severe. Mine was fairly mild. From that moment on I had echocardiograms every two years and fifty/fifty chance that my children would get it. So my two oldest have it, my youngest does not.

My advice to women would be to stay focused on what your actual goals are. I kind of crawled my way around because of my experiences, and didn't really get my act together career wise until I was in my 30s which is hard because I should be skating right now and I am not. But that would be my advice is to do as much of that when you are younger, so you can establish yourself and then actually enjoy the fruits of your labor. I have three great kids, absolutely blessed and as a single mother, I am very proud of that, and they are all doing the right thing. I think education is key in stability, and the other thing is never be afraid to talk about your issues because it can affect your life dramatically, if you don't.

Linda St. John
Age 49
Interviewed on November 13, 2013 by Emily Parravano and Caitlyn Thompson of Assumption College Overseen by Profs. Leslie Choquette and Professor Allison Meyer, Assumption College

I [finished] college and got this job in Pittsburgh. My job was basically watching the Proctor & Gamble products on all of these television shows, timing how long the product was on the air, then going to an advertising book, figuring out how much money Proctor & Gamble saved from a public relations perspective, by having their product on the air. It was totally boring. I had no interest in it. I kind of hated it.

And then, something wonderful happened. I got laid off from my job. My sister happened to be living in Worcester. So, [being laid off] led me here, and it really led me to human resources. One of the most difficult points in my life turned out to be something really positive because it led to where I am today.

I stayed [in Pittsburgh] a little bit longer and I went out and just got some temp jobs. I got to work at a whole bunch of different companies and I did lots of different things. They weren't high-level jobs at all. But, you know what? I was enjoying it. I saw the people who at that time were called placement coordinators, but they were recruiters. And they would interview all the people coming in, they would talk with all the companies, and then they would match up people for the jobs. They were helping people, they were working with companies, and I thought, "That looks really fun." When I moved here, my first job was as a recruiter at Fallon Clinic, and it's because of all that had happened. And that's how I got into human resources.

[Now] my official title is senior vice president and chief human resources officer [at Fallon Community Health Plan]. I'm responsible for running human resources. So, that's all about compensation, benefits, employment, recruiting, employee relations, organizational learning and development. I have people on my staff now who run those departments, but I'm responsible for all of that. I'm a member of the Senior Leadership Team, and I report to the president and CEO [Chief Economic Officer]. I'm helping to run the company with a senior group of people doing the same thing. I work with people responsible for sales and marketing, the chief financial officer, the chief operating officer, the chief strategy person, the chief communications person, the president of government affairs, and the president of the company. And, we're all trying to achieve our strategic plan, and move our company forward.

I started at Fallon Clinic as a recruiter. As a recruiter, I worked in human resources. I was responsible for interviewing people and placing people in the right job. You have to learn about the person. The person has to learn about the company, and the job, and the manager, and all that has to be the right fit.

We merged with Saint Vincent Hospital, and that was pretty exciting. You have to try to merge cultures and my boss at the time did something really neat in the world of mergers. He told all of us that we were going to move over to the Saint Vincent Hospital Human Resources Department. When you do a merger, it quickly becomes us them, we they, and he got us together as a department right away. I think that was really smart. It broke down a lot of barriers. My boss came to me and said, "What do you think you'd like to do? You've been recruiting for a while." I said that I'd like to do employee relations. He said, "That will be your new role when we move over to the hospital." So, when I went over to the hospital, I did employee relations for Saint Vincent Hospital, which was a 500-bed hospital of about a 1,000 employees. Fallon Clinic had about 600 employees at the time, and Fallon Community Health Plan had a couple hundred employees at the time, and I was basically the only employee relations person for that volume of people. It was a big job.

So, the hospital alone, employee relations was a full-time job. And, you had all levels of people, people working in the cafeteria, working in the laundry, all the way up through to nurses and administrators. So, you got to see a vast array of humanity. That was very exciting.

I saw a job posting here at the Health Plan that was for provider relations, and they were requiring a master's degree. So, I had just gotten my MBA [Master of

Business Administration] in health care and I thought, "Well this might be good." While I've worked in the same environment, the environment has changed so much that I feel like I've worked for several different companies throughout my career. I got the job, and I left human resources, and I went over and worked in provider relations. Turned out that I didn't love provider relations. It just wasn't the right fit.

The folks at the clinic called me and said, "Well, how are you liking it?" And I said, "Well, it's OK, but I think I've really learned that I'm a human resources person." And they said, "That's great because we're splitting [from the Health Plan and the hospital], and we want you to come back."

So we all worked it out. I went back, and I was really happy to be back. I got a new boss at the time, and it was a woman who just became a tremendous mentor to me, and really allowed me to grow even more. I think that what's really nice about my career is people have really given me an opportunity to explore, try different things.

The work here has meant a lot to me. I've learned that I can do it, and I think I've learned that I can do it very well. I've built a fantastic team of people who I work with where the fit is everything. We learned how to be a team, how to communicate, how to work through conflict. I've also proven to myself that I can be a good colleague to the rest of the senior team, that I can contribute to the business, and I've learned that I can work pretty successfully with the president and CEO of a billion dollar company and support that organization.

I think one of the ways that I found success in my life is really first of all getting to know myself, taking some real time getting to know what was important to me. I knew a lot about the practicalities of the job, but a couple years ago I wanted to learn more about the theory. I wanted to learn about organizational design and development. So I went into a blended program at

Massachusetts School of Professional Psychology that was a 10-month program. A lot of it was learning about master's level organizational psychology and the impact of psychology on an organization—how anxiety affects people and organizations. And we're in a pretty anxious time right now with the economy, and I realized if I'm really going to help people and help the organization, that I needed to go get some of that theory. Then when I moved into this job, [it was] a culmination of everything that I had done over my life. I believed in working hard, I believed in surrounding myself with good people, the whole "fit" thing.

I think advice that I would give is that it doesn't happen overnight, that it's a process. Find out what your values are, what's really important to you, and stick to them. The other thing is, find a mentor. Look to some women who maybe are a few years ahead, or are doing what you might want to do, or have values that you want to ascribe to and seek them out. I had women who were mentors. I listened, and I paid attention, and I saw what they did, and then I decided on my own path.

Nancy McBride
Age 65
Interviewed on March 26, 2008 by Tara Fountain and Christina Gagliardi of Assumption College

I was married to a clergyman, and so we moved around a lot. He'd been in trouble for a while with a brain disorder and bipolar. And he wasn't able to function, so he left. I never had child support or alimony, nothing, so that was huge. And that's what drove us into poverty quickly and no matter what little jobs I could put together they hardly competed. But it was at the time when my mortgage was low, so I could pay for that with a few of my jobs, we couldn't get food stamps because we owned a car. And it was so humiliating. It was traumatic financially as well as emotionally.

But I did make, through my radio program, one friend who introduced me to a group of single people, with whom I became good friends, people who were going through the same kind of thing as I was. There was a lot of support, and laughter, and potluck suppers [laughs]. Yes it was hard. I was still a single mother, but I couldn't look at it as a problem, I had to look at it, "OK, what am I going to do next?" So I don't think I processed a lot of the trauma, from one job to another, to my husband leaving, I didn't have time to process it.

I did [find it challenging balancing work and family], because I didn't have a role model for that in those days. I had not developed a career. I had a lot of interesting jobs. I had a radio talk show for a couple years, and from that I met people who hired me at the aquarium at Niagara Falls. And I learned from every one of these jobs. I worked for a theater [in] retail sales, then I started public speaking. And then I started working for colleges. The first college I worked for they wanted a PR [public relations] director and an alumni director, and they had never had either. And so they asked me what I would do, so I made it up! [Laughs] Just like I made up how to be a radio talk show host. I learned to get the job, then find out how to do it [laughs].

You don't know anything about yourself until you say, "How did you raise two children and work through that environment?" There was a lot of learning how to deal with poverty, and that is a really good thing because then if you're ever poor again, it's no big deal [laughs]. It's not so traumatizing. But you just put your feet down, and get up, and do it. I've learned something from every job. But I don't think I ever considered I had a choice, and I had nobody to bail me out.

Wooo hooo! [Laughs] I am [enjoying retired life.]. I am finding I had to be careful not to be too involved at first. I trained last fall as a standardized patient at UMass [University of Massachusetts] Medical School. I play the role of a sick patient for a specific medical student who is trying [to develop] skills for interviewing and messing up all over the place [laughs].

I've been teaching twice a week, no pay, English as a Second Language to students who have some ability with English, but no depth. I provide the depth in the class and the cultural connection for that. I'm loving it. I've been taking them on day trips. They are from Turkey, Vietnam, Puerto Rico, and El Salvador.

I'm involved in the Heifer Project pretty heavily, up in Rutland. I'm a cashier for the pancake breakfast on Saturday, and I do group tours, and I'll do heavier training for orientations. Heifer Project has been very important to me. I would say that I am careful not to overextend myself, and over the years I have learned how to say no. And the world won't collapse.

And I'm doing my art, and loving it, and people like it. Well, I don't care if they like it or not, but I'm happy with it. I'm finding out a lot about how I learn and I don't learn by [following], "Today, we're going to do this." I learn by getting in a big mess and saying, "What's next?"

I've done a lot of amazing travels around the world and met fabulous people, I've certainly lived an interesting life so far, but it's not what it's all about. The bottom line is the present, and enjoying this conversation with you and just appreciating the present. There have been times in my life where I can't help but think, "If I die now, it'd be OK." I had a couple of big jolts. I was struck by lightning, as a child, through the telephone, and had a near death experience as a result. And I was off a cliff in a car hanging over the edge. I was swept away in a flood, a few other things like that in my teenage years, so I don't

179

really remember trivial problems [laughs]. But I think a lot of those kinds of [things] gave me an opportunity, not to lower my expectations of life, but to simplify them so that I can enjoy it, and dig deep, and not take for granted what people tell me. So that doesn't mean my life won't go down some more dark paths, and it certainly has, but I think it's the light at the end of the tunnel and the promise that you can get there.

Ann Louise Flynn
Age 66
Interviewed on March 21,
2006 by Alexandra Phillips of
Worcester State University
Overseen by Prof. Lisa
Krissoff Bohm, Worcester
State University

When going through public high school, I liked math and I liked sciences, and everybody was equal, and there was no issue of discrimination. This was in an era when there were many more all-women colleges, and it was also at a time when many fine liberal arts colleges were all males; they were either all women or all men. So I could have gone to numerous colleges if I wanted to major in education or nursing, but I didn't. I wanted liberal arts. I wanted physics or math. That pretty much geared you towards women's colleges in that era. So I went to Emmanuel [College].

I graduated from there and worked that summer at MIT [Massachusetts Institute of Technology] as a math analyst, and had a fellowship to St. Louis [University] for physics. Working at MIT was interesting, and I could have stayed, but again there was almost a sense of, "Well, it's a little bit odd to have this woman in this system," in that era. So I went on to St. Louis, and it turned out that I was the only woman in the graduate school class of physics. There was another woman, and she was a nun. There were 58 men, myself, and this nun. I was in situations where faculty would say, "Well, if there wasn't one person sitting in this room, I would be able to tell you this joke." At that time it was something like a little less than one-half of one percent of the physicists in the United States were female. So there just wasn't a lot of companionship or support. It was always, "You're the weird one." I would say it took more of [an] emotional toll.

I applied to become one of the RA's [resident advisors] in the dorm and they hired me. And that's really how I started to get connected into the social sciences. And then the following year I became the assistant director of the residence hall. [Then] they offered me the position of full-time dorm director. I took the dorm director position, completed my master's thesis, and then I was at a crossroads. Do I continue on in physics or make a change?

And I was having a good time doing the dorm work, and dating certainly was a lot easier then. [I wasn't] this weirdo, you know. I mean I could sort of downplay the physics and play up well, I'm just resident hall director. I thought, "Well if I'm going to be in this line, then I need to get some courses." So I was able to do the equivalent of the undergraduate major in psychology.

And Father George Drury from B.C.[Boston College] was out recruiting for a director of women's housing for B.C., and he had come up to St. Louis and interviewed me. I came back for an interview, and I found things discriminatory at the time at B.C. The women still were only in education and nursing. The women lived off campus, a mile off campus, and [they] paid more money than the men who lived in residence halls on campus. So I said, "For sure you don't want me because there's no way I can support this," and Father Drury said, "No, for sure we do want you and that's why we want you." And he was vice president of student affairs at the time.

Well, I did take the job. We ended up having a demonstration for bringing women on campus and for equal costs. So, the women and many men had a sit-in and we achieved that [laughs]. So that second year that I was there, women had residences on campus, and the charges were the same. Then the third year I was director of university housing, and there were numerous administrative struggles going on. And in the fourth year I was named dean of women—Arts and Sciences went co-ed [coeducational], so I was named dean of women. At the time, I was also going to school at B.U. [Boston University] to get a master's in counseling education. I was let go that year as was the foreign student advisor.

I was being fired because of what I stood for, but the way they presented it to me was they were having cutbacks, and so the first ones into a position were being let go. Well, I was in my fourth year, but it was my first year as dean of women. So I thought this was bogus, and then students heard about it and the students had a sit-in at the president's office and [laughs] that went on for a few days. They couldn't figure out how to get the students out of the president's office. They had to call me in on it to get the students out.

I hired an attorney, and I sued B.C. And so when I left B.C., the legal case was going on. And then I went into doctoral studies at B.U. I figured again if I'm staying in this field, I'm going to need a doctorate sooner or later. And the suit did finally get settled, and I won the case. They had improperly let me go.

I was completing my doctorate at Boston University, and a position opened up at [College of the] Holy Cross. I started working at Holy Cross in 1973 [as a] psychologist at the Counseling Center. When I first started in Holy Cross they had just gone co-ed. [Later] I was co-chair of the ten-year anniversary of [coeducation at]

Holy Cross, and we invited Gloria Steinem as the keynote speaker. And that created quite a bit of stress because Gloria Steinem was very supportive of women's rights and things like birth control and abortion. It was a great evening and students were up all night talking about the presentation. It influenced conversations in many courses the next day.

When I was at Holy Cross, I supervised some interns from the Rape Crisis Center. We had numerous programs to educate and teach women with respect to rape issues. I think rape in general, not only here in Worcester but across the country, is a difficult issue. If somebody brings charges of rape, to prove it in the court is very difficult. And if you have a judicial system on college campuses and bring rape charges there, again it's always the difficulty of evidence.

At Holy Cross I was [a] psychologist in the Counseling Center, then associate director of counseling, then director of counseling. I was at Holy Cross for 27 years, so that's a large span of work. After a couple of years of retirement, [I] did some consulting. More recently, [I'm] coming up on two years here at the United Way as the assistant vice president.

I think growing up in the family that I was in, that was largely male, going to public school, there was just always the sense you could—gender was not a barrier. I wasn't raised with the thought that gender was a barrier. And I encountered it really for the first time at St. Louis in physics, and became more aware of the conflicts of women in science, and knowing there weren't many women in physics or in astronomy.

Elizabeth D'Errico
Age 69
Interviewed on March 13, 2009 by Shaina O'Neil and
Katherine Gleason of Assumption College
Overseen by Profs. Leslie Choquette and Linda Ammons,
Assumption College

I always wanted to be a nurse, and my parents didn't have the money to send me to nursing school. So I got a job at Norton Company. I was a teletype operator at Norton Company, so we would send all these little telegrams. This was before computers came around. Then for fun we used to send—we used to exchange recipes. I always knew what the weather was going to be, because we had contacted people in Chicago. They would always tell us the weather and we always knew that if there was a snowstorm, we were going to get that weather within the next couple of days, because it always came east. So I went to work when I got out of high school. I graduated in '57, and then I went to work right away. I got a job at Norton Company and got married in '59 to my first husband, Richard. And I worked at Norton Company until I became pregnant with my first child which was in 1963.

I started there basically because I needed to work and so I started working there and then I got pregnant. It was a long time before I got pregnant; we waited almost four years I think. Things just weren't happening so I had to wait that time and then had my first child in '63. And then before I knew it, I got pregnant again with my second child in '64, and then came my son in 1966. And then I became a widow in 1974. Prior to that, in those days, your husband, or my husband, didn't believe that a woman should work so I didn't work. And finally, things were— we were living from paycheck to paycheck, just like everybody else. And I said, "Gee, I'd like to go and just get a job working at Christmas time." So that's what I did.

I worked at Spag's in the toy department. After that I said, "Gee, I really want to work," because now I got spoiled and liked this spending money that I had. So I got a part-time job at Friendly's, which is still open at White City. I worked there until—well 1974 was when my husband died and I said, "Well, now what am I going to do?" I needed to support my family. I said, "You know what, I'm going to do what I always wanted to do." So that's when I decided to become a nurse.

I went to Hahnemann [Hospital] for an interview and the girl there said, "You know what, Betty, why don't you get your feet wet and go take a college course at Quinsig [Quinsigamond Community College]?" So there I went and did chemistry. I was fine. I breezed through that because I remembered. I needed a lot of help with Chemistry II, but I did pass it. And that gave me the confidence to put an application in to the Hahnemann School of Nursing, and I was fortunate enough to get accepted. I did three years of school there and with that, I went to Worcester State College and I think I did one year at Worcester State. And it was very hard, it was very difficult because I had three children, so my bedroom door was always closed, but I was home. They were going to have a coming-out party for me when I finally graduated. I graduated the same year from nursing school—which was in 1981—that was the same year my daughter, my older daughter Pam, graduated from high school.

The role of women has changed as far as working, I think, because as I said to you before, my husband didn't think that a woman should work and I went right along with him. My job was to stay at home, cook the meals, do the ironing and the washing, and doing everything that a woman was supposed to do in those days. But times have changed. When my daughter first got married, I went to visit her and her husband said, "Excuse me, I have to go get my shirts out of the dryer." So I said, "My God," I said to my husband, "Can you imagine she doesn't even do his shirts?" And then I went home, and I thought about it, and I said, "You know, I'm working full time and I'm still doing all this." My role had to change and I changed. I changed the way that I looked at things. If I'm working full time and he's working full time, we have to do some of these things 50/50. So I guess I came a long way.

I always tell my children that you should always get a good education because you never know when you're going to need it. I was a widow in my thirties, had three children to bring up. So you basically need to get your education, get a good job, just so that you can survive today. So that's the advice that I would give to anyone.

Maddie Levine
Age 80
Interviewed on November 15,
2006 by Christine McLaughlin
and Shannon Murtagh of
Assumption College
Overseen by Prof. Brian
Niece, Assumption College

My mother was born in that part of Russia that changed frequently between Poland and Russia because it was on the border. She came [here] when she was 18 or 19 years old. She left three sisters in Russia; her parents had died.

And she came and, of course, had no money. And what she did was, she got hired as a, I guess as a babysitter, a nanny to people who were going from Russia to the United States. But they went—instead of going the normal way, going west and going across the nation, they went east and went on the Trans-Siberian Railroad. For months, and it was horrible, and ended up in Japan, where they had to burn all their clothes; they were lice-ridden. It was a horrible journey, but she said Japan was wonderful because it was so clean, everything was so clean. They cleaned themselves up and I know she got on a boat, and I know she went from Japan, some port in Japan, to Hawaii. How she got to New York, I don't know; the story ends there. She finally brought her three sisters over.

[My father] was sent here to learn a trade, and to avoid the [Russian] army. He had a relative here who took him in, and he was a dental technician. And he went into the [United States] Army and became a citizen that way. He met up with two other people and started a dental lab. And they were very successful. Mostly he was fun loving; he loved a good time. My mother was more intellectual. There were three children, I'm the middle child. We all felt that we were our father's favorite, [laughs] and I don't know who was, but I really think it was me.

My husband's name is Stanley, and we knew each other in high school. I thought he was so, so handsome [laughs]. I thought I would never, ever date him. But after the war, all these young men came home, and I think they were looking for wives at that time. Here it is 59 years later [laughs] and we're still together. I have five children, and I will now have 11 grandchildren.

I must have been about 45. I decided to go back to school, and I went to Clark [University]. They accepted all my credits from junior college. I went nights, and I loved Clark. I went with a friend of mine, and we had a wonderful experience.

I think it was an age thing more than just being a woman. People, friends would say "Oh, aren't they cute? They're going to school." That was a long time ago, now [older] people go all the time. But it was so patronizing, so demeaning, and here we are working our little butts off [laughs], and people are talking to us like we're silly girls.

It must have taken me about four years to get through the two years. I graduated, and then, with the same friend, said, "Now what are we going to do?"

[Laughs] We decided that we were going to get a master's in social work.

So we applied, got into BU [Boston University] School of Social Work, and went. And [I] graduated when I was 50. And I thought I could never get a job, but people were looking for stable people. I was in the community, I wasn't going to get married, I wasn't going to have a baby! And I wasn't going to move away. So, I had my choice of jobs, and I worked at Worcester Youth Guidance for about seven years, and then went to the Jewish Home for about another eight years. At least in my day, most of the big, good administrative jobs in social work went to men, not women, and the field was mostly women. I shouldn't say the good jobs, but the well-paying jobs.

And then I retired [laughs]. Oh, I love retirement! [Laughs] We're having a great time. W.I.S.E. [Worcester Institute for Senior Education] takes up a lot of time. Actually my girlfriend and I were the two who began the process. We retired [and] we said, "Well what are we going to do now? We have nothing to do." We had heard of a program at Harvard [University], it was a learning in retirement program. A man who was in the Harvard program came, and spoke to us, and we got very excited about trying to start a group here. [We] contacted all the colleges, and the consortium, and did all kinds of things. The dean of Continuing Education [at Assumption College], Charlene Martin, [knew] about learning in retirement, and was looking for a community group. And so when the consortium got together she said, "Oh-ho! Here you are, a community group looking for a home, and I've got the home, we're looking for the group." [Laughs]

We had a program to introduce people to the idea of W.I.S.E. and we thought, "Oh let's hope a hundred people come, maybe fifty people will come." Well, we caused a traffic jam on Salisbury Street so many people were interested. And now we're up to over 400 people and we offer 60 courses a year. It was a hit! And people say, "What would I do with all this time [in retirement] if I didn't have W.I.S.E.?"

Erica Ayisi
Age 33
Interviewed on
November 16, 2014 by
Sharon Caulway and
Diana Waterman of
Assumption College
Overseen by Profs.
Christine Keating and
Leslie Choquette,
Assumption College

My parents are African immigrants who migrated here in the '70s. I always knew growing up that my immediate family was in Ghana, and I grew up very Ghanaian, very African in America. I grew up a Ghana girl in Worcester.

I was a very weird child, and my father had a very global sense of things and was very smart. I read *Newsweek* at 10, watched Jeopardy, I still do. I wasn't really into Barbies and things of that nature. I was always into the world, having a global sense of things and always wanted to be knowledgeable. I went to Burncoat High School and did the morning announcements on the speaker my senior year. We had a TV production show, and so I knew I wanted to be working in news and be a news reporter. And that's kind of what I set out to do. I [earned] a bachelor's degree in communications and I became a teacher. And I taught English for six years.

I taught at Burncoat, I taught at the high school that I went to so that was interesting in itself. I knew some of [the students'] struggles. I knew what it was like to have immigrant parents because I had immigrant parents. And no matter what country they come from, having immigrant parents when you're a first-generation, is very difficult. Everything is a first. Everything.

So it was good to be a Worcester Public School teacher and I did enjoy it up until year six [laughs]! Then I decided it was time to go. I had great experiences and unfortunate experiences. I had students die, I had students shot, I had students give birth [laughs], I had students get married [laughs]. It kind of seemed the gamut of urban education and the American youth.

And initially I didn't know what I wanted to do next. I called New York Institute of Technology and they had rolling admission. And they also had a campus on Long Island that had a news TV station attached to it, so I wouldn't have to apply for an extra internship and maybe not get in. I could start practicing and learning how to be a reporter right away.

I felt I got what I wanted. I wanted a whole new life—I wanted to be a different woman. So yeah, it was great. I went to school, and then I would go to Long Island about once a week. I learned how to shoot, write, and edit, and I got to do that right away which was very important.

I wanted to be an international journalist, so I called up some family in Ghana to see if anyone knew anyone at any of the local stations there and I had a cousin that did, so I interned for eTV Ghana for about a month and just packed up and bought myself a ticket, and was an intern in Ghana and stayed with family. So I finished my degree and then I decided to go to Ghana! It wasn't an internship, it was a job, and I was going to be a full-time reporter in Ghana.

And it was good, it was bad, it was ugly, it was challenging. My first day, my first news assignment was interviewing Bob Marley's wife, Rita Marley. I covered a lot of sad stories on malaria, cholera. There was a cholera outbreak there at the time. A lot of health and sanitation stories with the filth—the city was filthy. It's very filthy, and overpopulated, and dirty. I covered everything, health and fitness to politics. I saw the most extreme level of poverty.

I didn't think I would have the challenges that I had with having African parents, but I realized I grew up African here [in the United States] and, and that's very different [from] how women are socialized [in Africa]. I was kicked out of a bar because they thought I was a prostitute. Just because I was alone. In America we are socialized after college you get a job, get good money, you get an apartment. In Ghana, there's no sense of independence, or of, "Oh, I have a good job, I went to school, I'm going to live on my own or with girlfriends." They don't do that. You don't leave your house unless you're married.

In Ghana you either get paid twice a month or once a month and we got paid once a month, [but] that almost never happened. But the final straw was two things. My father was very sick, and then secondly I was about five minutes late [for a meeting], and I grabbed a chair, and sat down. [The news director] said, "Erica you're late so stand up." I said, "Excuse me?" He said, "You're late, stand up, that's your punishment for being late," and I said, "No, no, I don't have punishments." [Laughs] I felt very embarrassed, probably one of the most embarrassing moments of my life, for someone to tell me to stand as a punishment because I'm late. And I packed and I came home.

I got accepted into the NBC [National Broadcasting Company] page program. Thirty years old giving tours of an NBC building. But I was humble, I never ever complained. So a full-time job came up with the Nightly News with Brian Williams for an editorial assistant. I got hired to work for Brian Williams. I wasn't reporting, but I—you can't say no to something like that.

You're going to learn, learn with the best of the best that do it.

My official title was an editorial assistant for Nightly News with Brian Williams. I did everything from finding stories, finding people to interview, pre-interviewing people, going out on shoots, doing stuff for the website, writing stuff for the website, just the whole entire gamut of news, other than being the face of the story. I did all the work behind the scenes for the story. About six or seven months into the job, my father died.

He died at home. I was just grieving and held the element of grief for a very long time. I just wanted to do nothing for a while and nobody understood it. I came back to Worcester and I did nothing for a year. I got hired in Worcester for Channel 3, Worcester News Tonight, and that's what I do now. I'm a reporter—I like to say journalist, but it's the same thing—for Channel 3 in Worcester. I am on air five days a week.

I am [happy in this job] I know how to do this job. I'm really a one-woman band. I drive, I write, I shoot, I edit, I carry my own equipment, I don't have a camera man, I do my own lighting, I do my own sound, I interview people. I come back and piece it all together and make it look pretty for 90 seconds on TV. But it's a good job. I don't plan to stay forever, but I'm happy with my job.

So it's kind of full circle. I never thought I would be living in Worcester, coming back. Never in a million years did I ever think that. I never even wanted to work in local news! I wanted to do international news, but the opportunity was here, and I have a place to live, and I think after you have all kinds of experiences, at least with the ones I've had, you learn what's important to you and what's not. I think it's individual for everybody. But here I am. So that's my life!

We are all here one time, and to wake up every day is a blessing. Maybe it's from living in Ghana with no lights and no running water, and some things become important to you. So, I'm very grateful. I'm very, very blessed.

Polly Tatum
Age 49
Interviewed on November 25, 2013 by Alexandra Furtado, Jennifer King of Assumption College
Overseen by Profs. Leslie Choquette and Allison Meyer, Assumption College

My maiden name is Polly Ann Jones and my married name is Polly Ann Tatum. I have been married, I'm divorced, [and I have] three girls. I was born and raised in Massachusetts, and I was adopted as an infant; raised in a Christian, African-American family. And when I was about 21 or 22, I found my biological family and have a strong relationship with them, and they're from Bermuda.

I think with any area, there are folks who are pioneers and who have paved the way for other women and there are opportunities, but you have to go out and seek those opportunities. My guidance counselor told me that I would make a good secretary. So I learned how to type on an old manual typewriter, but in general it made me feel like she didn't believe in me, and I'm the type of person who is very resilient. So if you tell me I can't do something, that's just going to make me try even harder. So I really didn't pay her any attention and forged my own path. I worked in all these different factories and realized that I didn't want to be doing this for the next 30 years of my life. Nothing wrong with it, but it was hard work and low pay. So I came to Worcester and started college at Worcester State [University].

I think I did three semesters there, and then met my former husband and had a child, got married, ended up stopping school for about a semester and working full time because I had this child I had to support. And then I went to a non-traditional college that incorporated work experience, so it allowed you to work and also go to school weekends, and have a family, and balance things. So I ended up getting my undergraduate degree at New Hampshire College in Manchester.

I think at the time I finished I might have had three children. I was working full time and going to school part time. It was intense. So my undergraduate degree is in human services. I went to Mass. [Massachusetts] School of Law for my JD [Juris Doctor], which is your first law degree. My youngest was five months old and I started law school nights, and I was working full time in human services. And it took me about three and a half years to get through law school nights and I finished in '94. The challenges were working full time, raising a family, having three children, my husband at the time was just new to the police force, so he was working nights, and just trying to balance everything.

It was a struggle. So from undergrad to law school because I went straight through, it took me 10 years; and anything worth having you fight for it, so that's what I try to instill in my own daughters. Once I finished law school, I took a job with the city of Worcester. [Later] I started my own practice.

I started my practice in June of '97, and I like to say that I work with the entire family. I do some adoption work. Of course, because I'm adopted, I certainly had an interest in that area. I do some divorce mediation work which is working with couples to help them divorce in a peaceful, private manner. I'm probably *the* most experienced divorce mediator in the county. I went back to school to get an advanced law degree, which is called a LLM [Master of Laws], in elder law and estate planning. I'm working with seniors who are either doing estate planning or are trying to qualify for Medicaid.

Most of my day is spent, not in court, but in the conference room working with families to help them find solutions to whatever their legal issues are. I have to say my favorite work is probably the adoption work, and helping people see their dream of becoming a family come to fruition. That's always a happy occasion.

I think the costs [of my chosen path] were the way I did it. I had children, and was raising them at the same time, and trying to go to school, and build a practice. I think the costs were we were always on the run, and I really don't know what they ate growing up. I have no idea how they got a meal. It happened! But I feel like it was all worth it; I don't think that I really lost too much. I wouldn't know how to do anything differently.

I have served on numerous nonprofit boards throughout the city of Worcester. One of my favorite organizations is Girls Inc., here in Worcester, and I was on their board of directors for a period of time. I coached Girls Inc., basketball for about 12 years. I loved coaching at Girls Inc. And now I'm involved with their Leadership Academy Program which is a 12-week program working with high school juniors and seniors. So it's a totally different age group. But I find that I like the direct impact of volunteering. I like the board work, too, because you can still make an impact on an organization. I've been involved with the YMCA and the Martin Luther King Business Empowerment Center. I've been involved with our [Worcester County] Bar Association. We serve about 1,100 lawyers throughout the county of Worcester and I'm a past president of that bar association. I was the third female president in their 125-year history and the first woman of color.

You have to choose what's important to you, not what somebody else is dictating what's important to you. You have to follow your own values. There is no blueprint for what life is going to bring you. Know that your life can go in a different direction and that doesn't mean that's good, bad, or indifferent. If you make a mistake, you grow from your mistakes. That's what life's about. We learn from that, and try to be good people, try to treat people well, and don't sweat the small stuff, for sure.

Wendy Wheeler
Age 52
Interviewed on October 23, 2006 by Erin R. Anderson of Clark University
Overseen by Prof. Deborah Martin, Clark University

[I was 17 and 19 when I had] my two children. I enjoyed being a mother. It was natural to me, I guess. After the second was born, I went to work. My first husband did nothing [laughs]. Within a year of going to work, that's when I left my first husband and met my second husband. And he did a lot. He helped raise my children, and we both worked, and he is excellent.

I went to work because I needed money to get by. I worked at Sprague Electric, right behind Great Brook Valley, so I could walk to work. I didn't have a car. I never got my license until I was 21. That was after I left my [first] husband. And Sprague Electric, I worked there for five years. Then I stayed home for another five years. That's when my [second] husband decided he'd buy a small business. We figured a place like a breakfast-lunch is just common sense, so that's what we did. And we found one next to Clark University. To just cook—cook, make people's meals, make them happy, I enjoy that. Oh, I've cooked all my life. When I was nine years old, I knew how to cook for nine people. My father taught me how to cook.

Oh boy. [Starting Wendy's Clark Brunch] it was stressful at first! You're cooking right in front of people. I had to learn not to think about anyone watching me, and just do it. My dad was always there helping me, and teaching me to relax because he came to work for me, too. And he helped me there. And it was so much fun after I got going. It was like everyone that came in was your family. Everybody knew each other. Everyone was friendly. And they actually started calling me "mom." They said, "You're like my mom when I'm away from home! You come and take care of me and you feed me!" And I started naming my breakfasts after the kids. So the specials had their names on them. They loved that. One of the examples was four eggs on a hamburger, with bacon, on a bulkie. We called that "Shep's Special," because his name was Shep [laughs].

[One morning] my husband went in by himself at 4:30 because we opened at 5:00. And you'd go in get everything going, the coffee, and everything. When he got there, there were so many kids outside waiting to get in the restaurant he couldn't believe it. He was panicking. They were up all night *studying* so they were all hungry! [Laughs] But they all just started making coffee, writing down their orders, giving their orders. They just kept coming, and taking the food, and doing the work, and doing it all for themselves, and it was wonderful. They were even running the register! [Laughs] He trusted them because we knew them so well.

[My husband and I] bought it together, but it was in my name. And I was there all day and he would help me at night—come help me close up, clean up, and start preparing for the next day. You always prepared your home fries and your bacon and your sausage for the next day. You precooked it all. He worked at Sprague and when he got out, he'd be over to help me by about 4:00. He'd come and scrub my grill, and I had a couple of Clark students that would help. We were open every day of the week. Seven days a week. It's a lot of work. We didn't take vacations. We bought it in 1984 and we sold it in 1987. My two daughters did everything with us. And they waitressed. Boy did they love that on the weekend! They could make a hundred dollars a day waitressing and they were 14 and 12 [laughs.] Oh yeah. It was a family atmosphere. Definitely. And then I did my bookkeeping every night. I had to learn that.

Being out with people [was the most enjoyable]. Being able to cook their food and make a really beautiful plate of food and they could really enjoy it. Everyone liked their food. That's a good thing. They say that most people starting their business are in debt for the first three years to five years, and we were never in debt.

After we sold Wendy's, I was offered a job by one of my customers—said he needed a purchase and sales clerk in his business. I didn't know how to use the computer. He said, "That's alright, we'll just teach you." So I worked there for three years. After that, I got a job at Imperial Distributors. I did accounts payable. I worked there until I went to work for Webster First Credit Union. After I left there, that's when we bought another business! I had Family Kitchen up on Hamilton Street. I found working for myself wasn't as stressful as working for someone else.

The difference starting [Family Kitchen] was that I knew what I was going to do. I knew what I had to do, and I just went in there and did it. We decided to make a *lot* of unique things. Different types of omelets and scrambles were our specialty. People just loved it. And we had a taco omelet. We had the chili and cheese omelet.

And my husband came up with this idea—he said, "What about a pizza omelet?" It was delicious. It was *very* popular.

Maybe I regret the fact that we didn't do a lot of family things when we owned a business. When you own a business, it's a lot of work and it is seven days a week. And my children missed out on any kind of family type trips or anything like that. So maybe that's one of the things that I regret, but I think that's the only thing. I think having your own business and working hard—I think it *taught* my children a lot. It taught them how to be responsible, and gave them a lot of experience for their future. I'm proud that I was able to run a business, and it always had a profit. That's really something to be proud of. And if you just have confidence in yourself, you can do it. I tell my children and my grandchildren that you don't *have* to have a college education to have your future work for you. You just have to work hard, and be determined, and you can be whatever you want to be. College makes it a little easier, yeah.

Louise Carrol Keeley
Age 56
Interviewed on November 5, 2008 by Amy Chiasson and Jessica Jané of Assumption College
Overseen by Profs. Regina Edmonds and Maryanne Leone, Assumption College

        I   was   born   in
Honolulu, in Hawaii. My dad was in the [United States] Air Force and so he was stationed there after the Second World War. I was in three different second grades. I went to third and fourth grade in Germany. And I loved

Europe! Loved it! To this day I love it! Loved that experience. And then we moved back to Andrews Air Force Base, and I lived there from fifth grade all the way to high school. So I've lived lots of places!

I went to Marquette University, which is a Jesuit school in Milwaukee, Wisconsin. And I went there from 1970 to 1974. I then went right after that to Boston College. So I got my MA [Master of Arts] and PhD [Doctor of Philosophy] from Boston College after many tortuous years. Those were not the best years of my life because I worked so hard. My dad used to always say, seriously, if I brought home a 99, "What happened to the extra point?" My mother would say, "A C is just as good as an A if you had fun getting it!" And so I didn't have enough of my mom in me, I had too much of my dad, and so I worked very, very hard.

I finished [graduate school] in the spring semester of 1983 and in January of that year my husband and I became engaged. I was trying to find a job somewhere locally, and it's hard enough to find a job in philosophy. And Assumption [College] had a position. And just by—again I'm going to call it the grace of God—I got this position. I got married when I was 31 years old, and my husband was 33. It was a first marriage for both of us, and we will be married 25 years this December. And so only once, and the four children are the product of that marriage.

Work is not my first priority. It's a really high priority for me, but it's not my first. To be honest, I know lots of people will disagree with me. My first priority is my relationship with God, my second is my family, and my third is my professional life. And to be honest the reason I don't always live them, is because God often takes a back seat to my family. It was really, really imperative to me that I be home with my children. I had my children late, and I came back to work half time teaching a couple of courses. I would rush back to the house, nurse Matt, rush back here [to the campus]. And I remember thinking this is ridiculous. Something in my soul was just torn. I was pregnant with my second son, Austin, and I was up for tenure, and I just said, "I can't do it, I don't want to do it." I could have done it, but I didn't want to.

And my confidante here on campus said, "Just get tenure." And I can honestly say at that time I didn't care if I got tenure or not. I got tenure, and so I asked for a leave, and they gave me a year. And I had the second child, but I just kept asking for a leave. And they kept giving it to me. And then I thought, "I'll ask for two years," and they gave it to me. It honestly is one of the greatest gifts of my life. And I would have quit if they hadn't given it to me.

So I was home with my kids for 11 years. And those were not the easiest years because I was—we were poor. I taught in Continuing Ed [Education]. At that point in the evening my husband was home. So I would be with the kids all day, run and teach a course for $3,000, come back. But my kids either had dad or me with them. I am immensely grateful. Joe Hagan, who was the president then, thought [giving me the leaves] was compatible with the family values of Assumption [College]. I feel like I've had the best of both worlds—at a cost, but still.

No we didn't have a [maternity leave] policy then. It's hard to imagine, back in the day there weren't any women in academics. For 23 years I was the only woman in my department. Women were rare and women who got pregnant were even rarer and rarest of all. Many faculty women—and again, this is their right—wanted to have children and work, and more power to them. It's just not what I wanted.

To me, [success] would be living according to those priorities that I told you about, which as I said I don't always do. If anything I spend more time with my husband and family, in service to them, and I think that's really important, being with them. I love to go shopping with my daughter. I do love that. We have a blast when we go together. Professionally, I am pretty ambitious, or I have been ambitious. I wanted to become a full professor and I did, so I was happy about that. And I had this interior drive to excel that has fueled a lot of my life positively and negatively. But the priorities of God and family and friends and academics, that would be the most important for me.

Patricia True
Age 67
Interviewed on October 16, 2006 by Carolyn Kriso and Kristin Pancotti of Clark University
Overseen by Prof. Deborah Martin, Clark University

I was born in Worcester in 1939. I have one son. The first [time] I was married 21 years, and the second time was 21 days. Twenty-one is not my number [laughs].

Both of my parents worked in a factory. In fact, they both worked at the same factory. And after a while, my father was jealous of my mother because she started making more money. In my time, it was "men were 'this,' men were 'that.'" Not women. Women were to have all these menial little jobs.

Well, my mother ran the machines and my father just went around supplying the work to each person running the machines, and the person that ran the machines earned more money than the stockperson. He wanted my mother to quit her job and just live on the money that he made, but my mother was a very strong person and my mother would not leave the job. My father was very heartbroken and would never tell people that my mother was earning more money than him.

I first went to work when I was 14. In those days your parents had to sign working papers if you went to work and I was working at St. Vincent's Hospital, the old building, for 65¢ an hour. But I used to give all my money to my mother. I never kept my money until two weeks before my wedding.

Girls were treated different than boys. Girls were always in the background and the boys were up front. So, when you went for a job, you got some little paying job while a man got a better paying job! Even though I could be doing the same job as a man, you wouldn't be getting the same pay. No matter what kind of job I took, I never got the same pay as a man.

Many times I said, "If I can do equal work, why can't I get equal pay? Why does there have to be a difference? If we're both doing the same job and we're both putting out the same amount of work for the same amount of hours, why don't I get the same pay he does? It's not fair!" They just looked at me and laughed. They said, "That's how the system is." Well, the system is changed now.

When I got married to my first husband, we lived in Fitchburg. And then we moved back here and he got a job here, so it wasn't too bad. But then he lost his job. The day we both went looking for a job, I got a job and he didn't, and that really lit a fire. And for a long time, I worked and supported the family and he didn't.

We lived off of Cambridge Street, because he got a night job at Reed & Prince making boxes at night. We were across the street from the factory so that way he wouldn't have to travel to work. And then we moved off of Cambridge Street onto Hacker Court and when we moved there it seemed like—this was a private street; it only had six houses on it. It seemed like when we moved there, he could not find any work and I just kept working and working and working. Never ending. The reason why I don't work now is because I used to walk to work from Webster Square to near the Holden line, and I ended up having two heart attacks on the way to work. I used to say, "I'm going to work until I'm 99 years old." But that put me out of work at 40-something. What a slap in the face that is when they tell you, "You can't work anymore." I had all kinds of jobs. I drove forklift trucks and loader trucks; I drove trucks and delivered caskets down South. I did time in the military. I took a 13-week course at the Worcester Police Academy.

In those days whether the women were smarter or not, didn't make any difference. You stayed in the background. People would say, "Speak when you're spoken to, don't speak otherwise." But see that didn't work with me. I just said what I had to say all the time and if people didn't like it, too bad! [My mother] taught me to stand up for what I believed in or wanted.

I worked as a nurse's aide at St. Vincent's Hospital. I talked to the nun that was there and she said, "If you want to work here, we can teach you how to do everything." At that time the nuns ran St. Vincent's hospital. So, it was nice to be there with female authority. And it was great having a lady boss. Everything you wanted, you had to go and ask them, but it was nice having females run a business.

Let's see, I worked at St. Vincent's, I worked at City [Hospital]. Then I worked in different rest homes. I worked at factories. I worked at Parker Manufacturing on Washington Street. I'll tell you the one job I didn't like. I worked three days at a waitress job, and I left. And it was at the Corner Lunch. Policemen used to come in there for their meals. One day I was serving them their meals, and I had a necklace on, and I thought the policeman was trying to grab me. All he wanted to do was look at my necklace. I went *bam*. I hit him in the face and told the boss, "Goodbye, I don't work here no more." Just because I am a waitress doesn't mean you have the right to touch me.

I tried to work around [my son] going to school so that when he was home, I was home. I would work third shift, so by the time he was waking up, a lot of times he didn't even know I'd worked. He never knew his mother worked [laughs]!

Victoria Waterman
Age 51
Interviewed on October 22, 2014
by Andrea Burnette and Heather
Ewell of Assumption College
Overseen by Profs. Leslie
Choquette and Christine
Keating, Assumption College

I graduated in 1985 and I had my pick of jobs. I could really go anywhere I wanted; it was a very different economy. I did pick a good major [and] I ended up staying in that field for most of my career. Between grants and financial aid I graduated with very, very, very little debt.

I had been working for a bank as a teller for a couple of years, since my sophomore year, and when I graduated—they were a small savings and loan in Rhode Island—they didn't want me to go. I didn't want to leave. They didn't even have a full-time marketing person, so they created the position for me. I stayed, and the business really did explode quite a bit. This was in 1985, before the tax laws changed in '86 making interest on home equity loans tax deductible. My world changed overnight when that happened, and our business quadrupled overnight. It was called the second mortgage business, the home equity loan, and we were licensed in several states. Our business grew from 12 employees, when I started, to 400. We were nationwide at that time, so it was quite a ride. And I was there for a total of 12 years.

In my last job in the financial industry I was the director of marketing for a nationwide mortgage company and I was the casualty of the industry that went sour and my company didn't make it. I wrote an article *Stay or Go: What to do with your Home when you Divorce?* and my phone never stopped ringing. I said to my boss, "I think we're on to something here." I got a call from the newspaper asking if I would write a monthly column. So this happened very organically. I networked with real estate agents, divorce attorneys, mediators, and we created a whole network and we trademarked it. It was called Divorce Mortgage Resources, and we had an informal network of women helping women. If there was ever a doubt, I saw the magic at that point of networking and how good it can be. Since then, I live networking, I love networking, and it's critical.

I came to Worcester when I bought a local affiliate of Leading Women. Leading Women provides leadership training to women. I ran Leading Women in Massachusetts and I had clients ranging from midsize accounting firms to Fortune 500 companies.

When I was with Leading Women, I was the board president for Girls Inc., for three years. I became a strong pipeline of volunteers for Girls Inc. It's like quicksand, you walk in, and it just sucks you in. And that's it, you're done. So it's just such a fabulous place to be. [This work means everything to me.] Everything, everything, everything. I've always had this common thread in my career of supporting women, that's always been really important to me. [Now as chief executive officer of Girls Inc.] I feel like I'm preparing the next generation of leading women. I leave every day exhausted and exhilarated.

When you educate a woman, you educate a family. So that's important. [My advice to women?] I would say learn how to ask with no apologies. Get good at that because women really stink at that. First of all, we don't like to ask for help, and second of all, we don't know how to ask for help.

I guess I would say that if I were to describe my career in one word, it would be serendipity. The path that my career took, although I didn't realize it at the time, all led to where I am today. When this opportunity [as CEO of Girls' Inc.] opened up, I never saw myself in this role, even though I was the board president. Started the search, encouraged people to apply, and then I got a call from a critical person who asked me, "Why aren't you going for this job? If you threw your hat in the ring, the search would be done for me." That was a pretty compelling statement. It was so apparent to everybody, but me. And I was the obvious choice by so many people, and I didn't see it in myself. So I was grateful for someone giving me the nudge for that, and so it's good advice. Think about what people are telling you. They might see things in you that you don't see in yourself. I have no regrets. I've learned from everything I've done, and it's made me a stronger, better person. I've had a lot of bumps along the road, and they all made me who I am today.

Rosa Lee Timm
Age 34
Interviewed on February 13, 2010 by Tim Harrington and Brielle Hart of College of the Holy Cross
ASL Interpreters, Kelly Muskopf and Ruth Wilcox of Northeastern University Overseen by Prof. Judy

Freedman Fask, College of the Holy Cross

My name is Rosa Lee Timm. My husband's name is Damon. He can hear. He is an interpreter at UMass

[University of Massachusetts] Hospital. He came to teach kids how to juggle at the deaf camp and I taught acting and dancing. First we were friends, then we dated, and then we were married.

Yes, [pointing to her pregnant belly] it's my first child. This is week 33 that means seven more weeks to go. His due date is April 10. Honestly it doesn't really matter [if the baby is deaf]. All I want is healthy. My husband wants a deaf baby, but [even though] he can hear. He thinks that maybe with a deaf baby it will be easier for the three of us to communicate.

My family is really good. We were different. My father is White and my mother is Black. My dad's family was not fond of black people. My mother was the only deaf person in her family. So the five of us kind of separated from our respective families and became our own close-knit family. We had a strong religious upbringing. It was a very positive experience.

I was deaf from birth. My dad is Deaf and his family is Deaf, so I am from a family of many generations of Deaf people. It's hereditary. ASL [American Sign Language] is my only way of communication.

My experience as being Deaf was positive up until the point of working in the "hearing world." It's very frustrating. Before I worked here in Worcester I worked at a place where I focused on helping deaf children find places to go to school, get hearing aids, choose appropriate doctors, helping their parents learn sign language, explaining the best choices for their deaf children. But here, it's been a frustrating experience. Communication has been very frustrating because I didn't have proper interpreters or technology such as videophones, and I had pagers that didn't work. In meetings with all hearing people, I will raise my hand, wait for my turn, and everybody else would still be talking. Finally I have to bang on a table or do something to get their attention. It can be really frustrating. Communication was just fine when living with a Deaf family and going to a Deaf college, but now I am the only Deaf person and it's a little bit more negative.

When I was younger, I was home schooled. For college, I went to Gallaudet University and didn't like it; didn't like it at all. So I left. Two years later, I was ready to go back to school. I went to RIT [Rochester Institute of Technology] in New York; they have a Deaf college there, NTID [National Technical Institute for the Deaf]. I loved it there. I stayed and graduated with a BS [Bachelor of Science] in Social Work. After that, I went to graduate school. I studied to be a rehab [rehabilitation] counselor. After I graduated, I worked in a vocational school for two and a half years. I helped Deaf people look for jobs. Now I am self-employed.

If you search on Google and you type in my mother's name, a whole list appears with her name of all the things my mother has done for the Deaf community. She travels the world and tries to improve education for deaf children. If it wasn't for her, I just don't know who I would be. With her help I've really come into my own. Thinking about my identity, the first thing I would list is being Deaf. That is really important to me. Second would be [being a] woman. And then the last [identifier would be being] biracial. I don't feel White or Black. I feel like a mix, like I am both, equally both. So in order of my identity, I would list Deaf, woman, then biracial.

I've been involved in theaters since I was 14. About five years ago I started my one-woman show traveling around the country. My business has started to grow and I made a DVD. We sell that, and we contract with others for work, too. If someone is working on a project and they need someone to sign it, they will hire me. Do you know the Statue of Liberty in New York? They have a tour, but they don't have access for Deaf people. I flew to New York to sign [ASL] and [with] a new handheld video device, you can see me signing the tour—welcome to the Statue of Liberty!

I started [acting] because it was really easy to make friends. I really don't like to make small talk with small groups of people. Growing up I was really shy. I really like theater because I was able to express my opinion and perspective. And I can express my emotion without really having to explain myself. Through art, you can create something and you can leave it for people to ponder it and think about it. You know how some people go to the gym and work out? Well I write, and play music, and I express myself, my opinions, my feelings through theater.

[I performed in a theater group called] Dangerous Signs. We did all sorts of different things. Comedy, we signed songs, we danced. We traveled to New York, Canada, Maryland. There were seven of us altogether and we acted throughout our college years. My stage name is Rosa Lee.

My [one-woman] shows target Deaf audiences. My theatrical style is mostly comedy. I like to use technology and incorporate that in my shows as well. I try to make my show very visual. It's an art and I want it to be visual. I use a film. I am on the film, and then I stand on stage, and I converse with myself in the film. [The dialogue] goes back and forth. Sometimes I have an act where I am sleeping. And then I am standing on the stage, trying to wake myself up in the film. So I take a piece of paper, and roll it up, and throw it at the film. The paper hits me, and I wake up, and I look down at myself on stage and say, "What's up?" Those kinds of things make it fun.

Acting has given me confidence. I'm very proud that I did the one-woman show. When I first started, I was afraid. Then I had a conversation with myself and I told myself this is a challenge for me. If I want to be strong and develop confidence, I have to just go ahead and do it anyway. It doesn't matter if the Deaf community likes me or doesn't like me. This is my work, this is my art, and I have to try. So I am proud of the fact that I did do it. I'm proud of the accomplishments that I made from then to now. And now I am here still standing strong. Yes, very proud.

Kathryn Tsandikos Interviewed on March 13, 2013 by AJ Efstratios and Tom Lomenzo of Assumption College Overseen by Prof. Carl Keyes, Assumption College

My name is Kathryn Tsandikos, [and I'm the co-owner of Coney Island Hot Dogs]. My father is a Greek Orthodox priest, retired. He went to Helena College which is a Greek seminary, became a priest, and served a couple of different parishes. He ended up working here and running [Coney Island Hot Dogs] because of my mother. It's her parents who had it, and she's an only child.

My mother did not work here because my grandfather did not allow her to work. My grandmother worked. She ran the place, but he did not want his daughter to work. She got married when she was 20, married my father, raised three kids—raised us well. I have a brother who is a lawyer and I have a sister who is a psychologist. I went to Boston College, and then I moved to Washington D.C. for a couple of years. I just worked and had fun. After that, I lived in Boston for a couple of years, and then I moved back here and this was it.

Coney Island is a landmark. I love it, you know, the fact that my grandparents had it, the fact that my father worked here, the fact I can be here and kind of carry it on the best I can. People still talk about my grandmother, and she's the one who should be giving an oral history because she was remarkable. I don't hold a candle to her and maybe someday I will, but she was just incredible.

I went to college, I had other jobs. I don't know, there was something about this that I just kept gravitating to. There was nothing glamorous in any way. When I moved back to Worcester, I was going to go back to school to get my master's in teaching. If I was going to come back here, my father said I should do something. I shouldn't just do this, he wasn't happy with that idea. My college degree was sociology actually.

When I was in college, I thought I was going to get my master's in social work. I thought I might do this, I might do that. I just didn't know. I worked at the Ritz Carlton for a year, hotel sales. I just really did not know what direction my life was going to take. And I tried [working at Coney Island], and maybe this might not have worked. I think the best opportunity I had was working here with my grandmother and my father. And I think that's what made it fun. It was just fun. I loved coming here every day, and that's what it's really all about.

[Religion]. It's a big part, a really big part of my life. I was brought up with it, my father being a Greek Orthodox priest. His philosophy is "Love and Jesus." When he preaches you always love each other and love fellow man and that's what Jesus is and that's what God is, it's love. I mean you can't just go to church on Sunday and disregard it, it has to affect every aspect of your life, and how you live. My grandfather was really influential in building the church, the Greek Church here in Worcester, and then my father was a priest there. Other people will sit around and talk about the weather, my family talks about the church. It just becomes who you are. That impacts you and what you want to do in the future. I sing in the choir, I stay involved in the church, I try to bring my kids up in it because you want to carry that on. I think I've become more spiritual as I get older.

I was very involved in the Greek community because my father was the priest. A few days a week I would go to Greek school, then on Sundays I went to Sunday school, and I was involved in GOYA [Greek Orthodox Youth Association], and GOYA used to have dances all the time. And it was really fun. A lot of my friends were Greek, so we had the same schedules. We were Greek-American. I grew up near Elm Park actually, which is near the church. It makes me feel so old when I say it, but we were allowed to run around. Your mother didn't know where you were until you came home for dinner at night. So we would roam the streets, and we would ride our bikes, and we were at friends' houses, and nobody knew where we were all day long.

[When I was younger,] I played the piano. Your life gets so caught up when you have kids. My daughter was a golfer in high school, so I spent an inordinate amount of time with her and with golf. My son was involved in theater and speech and I spent a ton of time with him. I think I lost a lot of myself in those years. I'm looking for more to fill up my life now that they're gone. So, that's where I'm at [now].

Probably the three things that get you through life are: your family, your friends, and prayer. I mean success is not money. For me, it's having raised a family, that's been a success of mine. Success is having Coney Island continue, so being able to continue the legacy that my grandparents started. But I don't measure it in terms of monetary success, that's never been me, I just don't. And anybody who knows me, knows that's not what I do. But success is relationships, having friends. That's what it's all about.

Sharon Smith Viles
Age 73
Interviewed on October 24, 2008
by Caroline Walls and Kathleen
Fitzgerald of Assumption College
Overseen by Profs. Maryanne
Leone and Regina Edmonds,
Assumption College

  I was in nursing school in
Chicago, and in those days nursing school was off limits to
men. I had four roommates living in an apartment with
two bedrooms and a living room. He and his buddies had
blind dates with some women in the class ahead of me.
This I didn't know. He called her and she said, "It's really
nice that you're coming to Chicago, but I'm engaged. I'm
so sorry." [Laughs] So, what they did, they came into the
nursing residence, and picked up the house book. You
know what a house book is? Like a bulletin board, with a
list of pictures, but a list of the spring formal queen and
her attendants, and I was one of them. So they started at
the top, and they went down until they got someone who
would actually talk to them [laughs]. And I answered the
phone, and three of my roommates, we were all there.
They called, and they wanted to know if I and a couple of
my friends would like to come down, and meet three really
handsome Harvard men [laughs]. It was just hilarious and
the guy who called, they picked him to call because they
thought he was the smoothest [laughs]. And so we went
down, met them, and they said, "Don't you want to come
[out] for a ride?" So all the concerns and worries young
women have these days, we didn't. So we walked out, and
here's this gorgeous baby blue Pontiac Bonneville
convertible. My future husband slid in behind the driver's
seat on the driver's side and I said, "I'm taking him."
[Laughs]

The next day he called me and asked me to go out on a date. It was interesting because I was in nursing school; he was on his way to medical school. And I had sworn to my roommates and my parents that I would never marry a doctor, especially not any stupid idiot from Harvard. I still didn't know that it wasn't his car.

Raising five kids, well you didn't get any sleep, literally, literally you didn't. When I was pregnant with my first child, my husband was back in school and I was talking to the wife of a pediatric surgeon and it was a Christmas party for surgical staff. She was a little older; she had five kids under seven. And she said, "It's so nice to talk to someone." In those days everybody had very large families, and there was no work outside the house. You just couldn't, there was no daycare. Unless you lived next door to your mother, you had to look after your children. There was no possible way, it was frowned upon. I did a lot of sewing kids' clothes. I cut their hair. I canned fruit and vegetables; had a garden. It took all day long every day. It was tough, very tough.

My nursing diploma was from Northwestern University. I didn't get a bachelor's degree until I was in my mid-30s from the State University of New York and I got [it] in psychology. I decided I wanted to go into the seminary, so I started seminary. Around the same time my husband was hired to start a pediatric care unit at UMass [University of Massachusetts] Medical Center. I was in the middle of my course in seminary, and I came to this area. I discovered that I wasn't called to the priesthood [laughs], and I found a job right after I graduated with the local bank. Did that for a couple years and got a master's in psychology. I did my internship at UMass Medical in the Department of Psychiatry. One of the nurses found out that I was a nurse and she said, "Why don't you come and work for us?" So, I did. Part time. Twenty-four hours a week. And six months later she quit. I had two master's degrees, not a whole lot of experience in hospital in place,

215

but a lot of experience in counseling that I had done over a period of 10 years or so. I went from being the intern to the charge nurse.

That was a period of time when healthcare was changing. They were looking at the bottom line and not thinking much about quality. We had 14, 15 disturbed children between the ages of 2 and 16. We had three serious injuries to staff and didn't really have much guidance or direction. They were absolutely understaffed, and I just felt like I couldn't take responsibility for a center run like that. So I quit. And from then on I worked for a small private agency that placed disturbed kids in homes. I trained parents. I also did behavior modification to help structure the life of the child. I did that for three years. And then my husband was going to go on sabbatical, so I quit my job.

I teach two classes at the [Worcester] Art Museum, Oriental Brush Painting and Sumi-e Ink Painting. I've always taken art classes here and there, always loved art. In '91 I had an accident and couldn't work. So I took a class in brush painting and it was love at first stroke [laughs]. I've been teaching that class since 1999.

I'm on the board of trustees for Briarwood which is a continuing care retirement community. I just came on the Worcester Women's History Project board of directors. I've been involved with Abby's House. It started out as a shelter for homeless women. I spent nine years working in these shelters.

I think the first two years or so of working at the shelter were very eye opening, and I learned the value of providing whatever was necessary to make life a little easier for people through the hard times. A woman came into the shelter who had walked from California. God! She had walked from California? This was the '70s. She was running away from her life. Life must have been pretty tough. There have been many like that. I think the work I did at Abby's House is the proudest I've been. Women were struggling. And I think it's important to help in this kind of way, and it's something that the next generation needs to find in themselves to help others.

Melissa Gibson
Age 40
Interviewed on April 16, 2012 by Billy Gargano and Sean Henderson of Assumption College
Overseen by Prof. Carl Keyes, Assumption College

The time of my life that means the most to me, was when I lived on a farm with my family. I was probably 8 to 14. That was probably the best, living on the farm. My husband got a job at EMC [Corporation] and then I wanted to get into business. We looked around and found a good location in Grafton. I think Worcester is a great city. You can get anything you want, it's big enough to find anything you need, but it's still small enough that you feel a kind of easy access to anything.

I have a high school diploma, and then I went to Fisher College at night when I was having my third child. I got my associate degree in business and accounting. Last year I went back, thinking I could go for my bachelor's, and did online studies. I did probably about six marketing classes to make myself feel comfortable enough to open the next store. I wanted to have a better marketing basis underneath me, but a lot of my learning is just reading. I read a lot. I'm on the internet a lot. I'm reading, I'm educating [myself], looking at what other companies do, what other businesses do, how they handle things, and I implement what I think could work for me. I think sometimes hands-on, or just being observant, is more important than a college degree.

I was an all A student and I graduated with a 3.9 [average]. It was fairly easy to get my associate [degree]. I think because I had two little children at home, and I was pregnant, and then nursing in the end with my third child, that was probably the hardest part. You know juggling that part, life outside, because I didn't go directly into college after high school.

When we first opened in Grafton, it was just me. [My husband] still held a job over at EMC full time. He would come home and work from 5 until 11 o'clock at night doing construction. And I would do construction and build. We built that facility in Grafton ourselves. I got on the tractor and graded the stone. We did all the labor. About six months into the operation, I told him he either had to quit or I had to hire someone. So, they offered him a severance package because they were going to lay off some other [employees] and he said, "I'll go instead of them."

Well, [Gibson's Natural Pet] is more than a pet shop. We also do daycare and boarding and training, grooming at both locations. It's our ultimate goal to educate the pet owner that you don't have to break the bank to give good quality care to your animal. It pays for all my hobbies. I barrel race and rodeo so I have five horses and that's my fun, that's my release.

I barrel race with the National Barrel Race Association and I rodeo. Barrel racing is a cloverleaf pattern, so you come around, you go through one barrel, another barrel, a third barrel and then back. You're on a horse, and you're going as fast as the horse can go, and [making] the tightest turns you can make, and you stay on [laughs]. I'm actually state champion this year, and won the state year-end also for high points. So, I'm looking forward to this season. I've got three horses to ride, so we'll see.

I have cavernous angioma in my brain which is kind of like a blood clot but not. So I have eight blood clots in my brain, and I have lymphedema in my leg. My mother died of complications from the same thing. It kind of was the catalyst to do all this. It was like life is too short; live every day to your fullest; you have no idea what is going to happen. She went to the hospital thinking she had the flu. Nine months later she was gone, so you never know. So do what you want to do, what you enjoy, and don't take no for an answer. If you really believe that there's something you should do, just go for it.

I just did things differently. I got married right out of high school, I had kids right away. Do I wonder if I hadn't done that, would I have gone to a regular four-year college? If I had been through a few relationships and settled down, would things have been different? I'm sure we wouldn't have struggled the same, and we wouldn't have strived as hard to succeed. But I look at it as, what if you'd done it differently? I don't think I would be where I am though now, if I had.

Ellen Smith Dunlap
Age 63
Interviewed on November 7, 2014
by Vanessa Urbina and Mary Jo
Herlihy of Assumption College
Overseen by Profs. Leslie
Choquette and Christine Keating,
Assumption College

I went to the University of Texas in Austin, and I was married there. After my first husband died, I met my current husband, and we lived in Austin until 1983. When I came to Worcester, much was made about the fact that I was the first woman in 180 years to be the head of the American Antiquarian Society, and people were always asking me, "So what does it feel like to be the first woman president in the Antiquarian?" and I [would reply], "I've been a woman all my life, I feel the same way as I always felt." I have been a pioneer in my field in many ways, but [it] has been very rare in my career that I have felt singled out as a woman. A lot of times, I have been the only woman in the room, so I've been kind of used to that. Worcester had a woman mayor a long time ago, we have women city councilors, we had leaders in the nonprofits, there have been college presidents. I've been a part of the generation where acceptance of women in leadership positions is so every day that it's a little more difficult for me to give a meaningful answer to that question.

I would say that I was very fortunate in that my calling as a librarian and working in special collections, like this one [American Antiquarian Society], kind of found me as I found it. The University of Texas is a huge place; there were 40,000 undergraduates when I was there. I took a course in the history of aviation. You could either write a paper or spend a certain number of hours in a little library that was on the campus that was devoted to the history of aviation. So, I said, "I'll do that." And that little library was part of a big university library that has an amazing 20th century history collection and literature collections. And they got to know me. So when I was in graduate school, [I] continued to work there. And then after when I got my degree, I got a professional job there, and I became the research librarian there. And that was just one of the coincidences that happened and kind of shaped my career.

I went from being the airplane girl to being an assistant dealing with all the people who wanted to use the manuscript collection there. I found out what they were working on, and what materials we had that would fit their research needs. When they came from England, or France, or New York, wherever they were coming from, I would interview them. And then when their books got published, they would always acknowledge my help. It was sort of like doing vicarious research, but I was called a research librarian. And then, in 1983, I was asked to become the director of the Rosenbach Museum and

Library in Philadelphia, which is a rare book and manuscript library. And then I came here in 1992.

I have no regrets whatsoever. I have had a remarkable life, just because of the institutions I have been privileged to be associated with. Once when I was at the University of Texas, [I] talked to [former First Lady] Jackie Kennedy on the telephone, and then when I saw her at a memorial service in New York, when I was living in Philadelphia, I went up to her and asked, "Do you remember calling me at the University of Texas?" and she did. It was a unique experience. I got a hug from President [Barack Obama] the other day. We were at the White House. The Antiquarian Society was singled out for a National Humanities Award, a National Humanities Medal. I went on stage, and I shook his hand and said, "I'm from Worcester," and Obama said, "Oh my gosh, I was just there at the technical high school! It's an amazing place." I said "I was there. I saw you hug all those girls and my daughter thinks I've concocted this whole medal thing to just get a hug from you." And he laughed and gave me a hug [laughs].

I'm curious about thousands of things. It's great to be a librarian if you're curious about things, because you know how to find things out. I can't imagine doing anything else. I have to say I'm a pretty lucky person. Yes my first husband died, yes my father died, but I really have never felt that I have had really tough times. I have had challenging times: little baby, a new job, husband unhappy that I made him leave Austin, Texas, trying to figure out where we were going to live in a big new city, that sort of thing. I think I was so busy with the new job, [I] just didn't have time to wallow in troubles.

I also feel that when you're responsible for a big organization and lots of people's livelihoods depend on me and the success of this organization, I kind of have this responsibility not to wallow in any frustrations, shortcomings, or trials. And this institution is 200 years

221

old, and we have a lot of continuity to maintain, so it kind of puts whatever I'm going through in perspective, and I think that's useful to get a grip on what are the big issues here, not the little ones. Don't be limited by anybody else's opinion of you. Don't be stereotyped by anybody else's expectations. I think my advice to women is, believe in your superpowers [laughs].

I think that as I look back, trying to recreate the stories of my grandmothers, and great-grandmothers, and great-great grandmothers, of course I can see when they married, when their children were born, and when their children died. So much of the outline of the story doesn't talk about what they felt. It doesn't talk about what was in their heart, and I think that asking questions like that is fascinating to scholars looking back in time. Of course that's what our library is full of, but the stories that aren't there, the things that are not said, are the tantalizing stories. So getting people, getting women to be honest about and open about their inner thoughts, I think is the thing for interviewers to do.

INDEX

ABOUT THE AUTHORS

Maureen Ryan Doyle has worked as a freelance writer for many years and is also the owner of a small property management company in Central Massachusetts. She was the winner of *Good Housekeeping Magazine's* New Traditionalist writing competition. Maureen  earned her BA degree in history from Assumption College where she was a member of the first undergraduate class of women. She received the Outstanding Alumnus/Alumna Award from Assumption in 2013. She has pursued graduate study at Emerson College in Boston and Oglethorpe University in Atlanta. She and her husband, Francis X. Doyle, reside in Holden, MA. Their family includes their daughter, Maryssa, and son and daughter-in-law Colin and Dani Doyle.

 Charlene L. Martin, EdD has 35 years of experience in higher education. She is the former dean of Continuing Education at Assumption College and the founding director of the Worcester Institute for Senior Education known as WISE. She earned her BA and MA from Assumption College and a doctorate in educational policy, research, and administration with a specialty in higher education from the University of Massachusetts at Amherst. She was an adjunct professor teaching higher education on the

doctoral level and her research and publications focus on educational opportunities for older adults in retirement. She and her husband, Jim Martin, live in Shrewsbury, MA.

Both Maureen and Charlene served on the Steering Committee of the Worcester Women's History Project and have co-chaired the Worcester Women's Oral History Project since 2008. In 2011 they co-authored *Voices of Worcester Women: 160 Years After the First National Woman's Rights Convention.*

We hope that you have enjoyed reading about some fascinating women of the greater Worcester area. These excerpts are taken from edited transcripts many of which can be found in their entirety on the WWHP website.

The work of the Worcester Women's Oral History Project is ongoing with new interviews currently being scheduled. Would you like to be interviewed? Do you know someone who would like to be interviewed? If so, please contact us at www.wwhp.org, click on Oral History Project, and then click on Share Your Story. If you would like to interview a woman for the Oral History Project you will find the required forms and interview guide on the website under Oral History Toolkit.

Made in the USA
Middletown, DE
28 October 2015